Measuring Native-Speaker Vocabulary Size

Measuring Native-Speaker Vocabulary Size

I.S.P. Nation
Averil Coxhead
Victoria University of Wellington

John Benjamins Publishing Company
Amsterdam / Philadelphia

The paper used in this publication meets the minimum requirements of the American National Standard for Information Sciences – Permanence of Paper for Printed Library Materials, ANSI Z39.48-1984.

DOI 10.1075/z.233

Cataloging-in-Publication Data available from Library of Congress:
LCCN 2020043798 (PRINT) / 2020043799 (E-BOOK)

ISBN 978 90 272 0814 9 (HB)
ISBN 978 90 272 0813 2 (PB)
ISBN 978 90 272 6029 1 (E-BOOK)

John Benjamins Publishing Company · https://benjamins.com

We would like to dedicate this book to our long-time colleague and friend John Read in recognition of his retirement, but mainly because of the quiet and thoughtful help, inspiration and support he has given to us over many years of working together. John's scholarly expertise is already well recognized in the field of language testing, but we hope that this book dedication shows that those who know him well value his friendship and have great respect for his scholarship.

Acknowledgements

Norbert Schmitt reviewed the book before publication and had numerous detailed suggestions for improving it. We are very grateful for his care, attention and expertise which greatly improved the quality of the book.

Part of Chapter 2 is taken from Nation, P., & Anthony, L. (2016). Measuring vocabulary size. In E. Hinkel (Ed.), *Handbook of research in second language teaching and learning* (Vol. 3, pp. 355–368). New York, NY: Routledge.

Chapter 3 is largely taken from the following article: Nation, I. S. P. (1993). Using dictionaries to estimate vocabulary size: essential, but rarely followed, procedures. *Language Testing, 10*(1), 27–40.

Parts of Chapter 4 are taken directly from Coxhead, A., Nation, P., & Sim, D. (2015). The vocabulary size of native speakers of English in New Zealand secondary schools. *New Zealand Journal of Educational Studies, 50*(1), 121–135, and Coxhead, A., Nation, P., Woods, L., & Sim, D. (2018). Group vs. individual: How administration procedure can affect vocabulary test scores. *New Zealand Studies in Applied Linguistics, 24*(2), 24–41.

Figure 6.1 comes from Diack, H. (1975b). *Test your own wordpower*. St. Albans: Paladin.

Figure 6.2 is from Larson, M. (2019). Estimating the vocabulary sizes of learners around the world. Presentation at IALLT 2019 (International Association for Language Learning Technology), Eugene, Oregon. <http://www.vocabularysize.net/iallt2019/iallt.html>.

Figure 7.2 comes from Keuleers, E., Stevens, M., Mandera, P., & Brysbaert, M. (2015). Word knowledge in the crowd: Measuring vocabulary size and word prevalence in a massive online experiment. *The Quarterly Journal of Experimental Psychology, 68*(8), 1665–1692.

CHAPTER 1

Introduction

This book tries to answer three questions.

> How many words does a native-speaker of English know?
> At what rate does a native-speaker's vocabulary grow?
> What influences the rate of growth?

The first question – *How many words does a native-speaker of English know?* – contains most of the methodological problems involved in answering the questions. What do we mean by *words*? What do we mean by *know*? What is *English*? Who is a *native-speaker*? How do we calculate *how many*?

These methodological problems are not easy to answer and ultimately involve decisions that some researchers and dictionary-makers will not agree on. What can be done in such circumstances is to make the research and reasoning behind each decision clear and to give some indication of the effect of making such a decision compared to a different decision.

The size and accuracy of any measure of vocabulary size depends on the size and accuracy of the answer to the question *How many words are there in English?* As we shall see, wildly incorrect answers to this question inevitably lead to inflated estimates of vocabulary size. Very conservative answers to this question lead to low estimates of vocabulary size. Knowing the size of the ball-park we are working in is inextricably linked to the answers we will reach about vocabulary size.

Why test the vocabulary size of native-speakers of English?

Typically, testing vocabulary size aims to find out how many words someone knows. Usually these tests measure the word form and a test-taker's ability to link form to meaning. One reason for testing vocabulary size is to find out how vocabulary grows over time, and another is to find out what knowledge is needed for reading, for example, and therefore inform the setting of classroom-based teaching and independent learning goals, writing teaching materials, matching readers to reading material at the right level, and curriculum design (Nation & Webb, 2011; Nguyen & Nation, 2011).

Table 1.1 contains examples of English words that are low frequency. That is, they do not occur often in texts, and if they do, they tend to occur only once, unless they are directly related to the topic of the text. Check to see how many of these words you recognise. Note that *paracetamol* is in the 15000–16000 column on the far right. Clearly this word would have a higher frequency in medical settings than in the BNC/COCA corpora.

Table 1.1 Examples of words at frequency levels from 9000 to 16000 from Nation's (2016) BNC/COCA frequency lists

9000–10,000	11,000–12,000	13,000–14,000	15,000–16,000
accede	refit	intension	paracetamol
legible	trowel	biochemist	caudal
chasm	prodigal	caw	troposphere
thermostat	mnemonic	balsam	cyan
attrition	yam	weevil	plantain
tawny	rootstock	narcissus	strophe
upkeep	askew	solenoid	toff
lubricant	sidelong	voluble	coterminous
chug	slob	conclave	rectilinear
hammock	marshmallow	crud	bisque

The history of vocabulary size measurement

Researchers have been actively interested in measuring native-speakers' vocabulary size for well over 100 years, but after applying even the most minimal criteria of methodological adequacy, there are only five sets of studies that are worth considering (Thorndike; D'Anna, Zechmeister, & Hall; Biemiller; Coxhead & Nation; Brysbaert et al.). We will carefully examine these studies in this book and present their findings. The other studies of vocabulary size are so fundamentally flawed that at best they serve as lessons about what not to do. We will look at these studies in this book and point out the lessons to learn. There are some studies that did not involve gathering vocabulary size data but which tackled important questions that clarified the methodology of the measurement of native-speaker vocabulary size (Thorndike; Lorge & Chall; Diack; Goulden, Nation, & Read; Nation BNC/COCA). For more on the BNC/COCA lists, see Chapter 5). We will also look at these studies in this book and evaluate their contribution. There is a very interesting set of native-speaker vocabulary size studies carried out in the early years of the 20th century which are largely single-subject studies of the vocabulary size and growth of very young native-speakers. Each child was closely related to the person carrying out the study, and the studies involved manually recording each new word the child produced. These studies rarely lasted longer than a few months because each child's spoken output around the age of four soon became too much for the researcher to keep up with. These studies provide a useful indication of the rate of growth of a young native-speaker's spoken productive vocabulary and are looked at closely in this book.

How many words does a native-speaker know, how quickly does their vocabulary grow, and what influences this growth?

Vocabulary size initially grows at a fast rate of around 1000 word families a year. This figure depends on the inclusiveness of the definition of a word family. A word family includes a headword (e.g. *measure*) and its closely related inflected and derived forms (e.g. *measures, measured, measuring, measurement* (Bauer & Nation, 1993). Vocabulary size growth typically slows as the number of unfamiliar words becomes smaller and the unfamiliar words are much less likely to be repeated. Herdan's Law (also called Heap's Law), which describes the likelihood of meeting unfamiliar words as the amount of the text increases, results in a similar curve to that showing native-speaker vocabulary growth (Keuleers, Stevens, Mandera, & Brysbaert, 2015) (see page 68). Vocabulary growth depends on opportunity to learn.

The rough rule of thumb for vocabulary size and growth for a native-speaker of English is as follows. Each year, from around the age of two, a native-speaker's vocabulary size grows at around 1000 words a year. Growth continues at around this rate until somewhere around the age of fifteen and unless the native-speaker engages in tertiary study or some other vocabulary expanding activity, the growth rate will slow considerably from then on.

Thus, to get a rough indication of a native-speaker's vocabulary size up to the age of around 15, take their age minus 2 times 1000. So, a 10-year-old will have a vocabulary size around 8,000 words (10 minus 2 equals 8, times 1000 equals 8,000). A five-year-old will have a vocabulary size of around 3,000 words (5 minus 2, times 1000). For the vast majority of native-speakers, their vocabulary size will be within plus or minus 1000 words of this average figure. A very small number will be outside this range. We will keep referring to this rough rule of thumb throughout this book, checking its accuracy and trying to explain deviations from the rule.

The variation in vocabulary size will be affected by the opportunity to learn new vocabulary, and this opportunity will be affected by socio-economic factors that affect the opportunity to gain new experiences both (1) real through doing lots of different things like going on outings, travelling, engaging with care-givers, and engaging in various activities, and (2) vicarious through reading, watching TV or movies, or making use of the internet. The quantity, variety and quality of the experience will be reflected in the quantity, variety and richness of the vocabulary learned.

So, vocabulary size is directly related to the amount, variety and quality of language-related experiences. The greater the amount, variety and quality, the larger the vocabulary size. Amount, variety and quality enable the learning conditions of meeting unfamiliar words, having repeated encounters with these words, and having high quality encounters through noticing, retrieval, varied meetings and use, and deliberate elaboration and analysis.

Factors including low socio-economic status, poor reading skills, and lack of access to technology can limit the amount, variety and quality of language-related experiences and can thus negatively affect vocabulary size.

In spite of these factors, native-speakers of a language with very few unfortunate exceptions learn their first language and, of course, the vocabulary needed to use the language. Even native-speakers who do not effectively learn to read develop substantial vocabulary sizes that follow the rough rule of thumb. Similarly, those who begin to learn English as a second language at a young age, when largely surrounded by the language and the need and opportunity to use the language, quickly become effectively native-speakers of the language, certainly from a vocabulary perspective.

What methodological decisions affect these size and rate of growth estimates?

The rule of thumb assumes that only single words are counted as words. It also assumes that words represent word families where words with the same word stem but with different affixes are counted as members of the same family as long as they share the meaning of the stem. The more inclusive the definition of the term *word family*, the smaller the vocabulary size estimate will be. There are four main assumptions for the rule of thumb:

1. Proper names, acronyms, transparent compound words, and various kinds of exclamations are not counted as words.
2. The rule of thumb is primarily an indication of receptive vocabulary size.
3. Not all words are known equally well.
4. When vocabulary size is being measured, each person will be provided with the support needed to truly engage with the test and show what they know.

A factor that affects the size and rate of growth estimates is whether we are measuring vocabulary size receptively (recognition of vocabulary in spoken or written testing) or productively (where test takers provide evidence of knowledge of the use of words in their own writing or speaking). Chapter 2, for example, focuses on the productive vocabulary sizes of young native-speakers, while Chapter 4 focuses on the receptive vocabulary sizes of young native-speakers.

Increasing vocabulary size

Vocabulary size is central to language use and is strongly affected by opportunities to participate in society and in family life. As we shall see, it is a part of a variety of causative chains, and functions as both a cause and effect in these chains. For example, vocabulary knowledge affects learning to read, and reading in its turn affects vocabulary knowledge. Vocabulary knowledge affects interaction with others, and interaction with others affects vocabulary size. We look at several such chains in Chapter 7.

It is important to see vocabulary size as part of causative chains because educational interventions need to take account of those chains. A good way of quickly finding out if someone knows about a particular subject is to see if they understand the topic vocabulary of that subject. For example, if you know anything about rugby, you will know the terms *punt, maul, ruck, conversion, scrum*. If you wanted to know what these terms mean, and as New Zealanders we consider they are essential knowledge, it would be foolish of us to try and teach you the meaning of these terms. Without understanding the game of rugby and its rules, the terms are meaningless. The way to learn what these terms mean is to watch games of rugby, even play games of rugby, discuss the games with others while watching, and learn the rules. That is, participate in the culture of rugby.

Vocabulary learning is affected by opportunities to learn and while the teaching and deliberate learning of vocabulary is one kind of opportunity, the opportunities to read widely and with skill, to watch informative programs on television, to interact with a wide range of different people, to travel, to learn new skills, to participate in education, to work, and to follow strong interests are all activities that will lead to vocabulary growth. The deliberate teaching and deliberate learning of vocabulary can play only a small role in a native-speaker's vocabulary growth. At certain times, as in parent-child interactions, at school, at university and when learning on the job, teaching and deliberate learning can play an important role. However, the deliberate teaching and learning should be a part of a meaningful wider learning opportunity. In the early stages of first language learning, vocabulary learning occurs through listening and spoken interaction. As children learn to read, then reading can become an important source of learning. However, it seems likely that the first 9000 to 10,000 word families are learnt largely through listening.

CHAPTER 2

The productive vocabulary sizes of young native-speakers of English

Although there has been a lot of research on the vocabulary knowledge of young native-speakers from different socio-economic groupings (Farkas & Beron, 2004; Rowe, Raudenbush, & Goldin-Meadow, 2012; Fernald, Marchman, & Weisleder, 2013), there has been little research on the total number of words that young learners know.

Measuring total vocabulary size

In this book we occasionally use the term *total vocabulary size* to distinguish tests that measure vocabulary size from tests that measure knowledge of a given set of words but which cannot be used to estimate how large a vocabulary a child has. In truth, no test is likely to measure the totality of a child's vocabulary. The term is used here simply to make it easy to refer to different kinds of vocabulary size studies.

In order to measure total receptive vocabulary size, a test needs to draw a representative sample of words from a well-defined population of words, such as a set of word lists or a dictionary. The proportion of words known in the sample can then be used to estimate the total number of words known in the population of words that they were drawn from. So, if a child gets half of the words in the test correct, then it is assumed that the child knows half of the words in the total population of words that the test-words were drawn from.

For very young children, rather than testing knowledge of words, some researchers have tried to note every word a child produces over a substantial period of time, the total number being their total vocabulary size.

Most recent research on the words young children know has not tried to measure their total vocabulary size but has simply compared different learners from different socio-economic groups or racial backgrounds or from different age groups, or has compared the same learners at different ages. Although the research described in this book is focused on total vocabulary size, the comparative research is of interest because it can show what test item types can be used with young children and can indicate the factors that are likely to affect total vocabulary size.

Measuring productive vocabulary size

The earliest published report on productive vocabulary size was by Holden (1875). In this study, Holden used a dictionary and counted the words that he thought he could use or had used, arriving at a size of 33,456 words. Holden did not look at his own written or spoken production and it could be argued that his test is a receptive test rather than a productive test. However, there is a long history of using the language produced by a particular person to measure their productive vocabulary size. Probably the best known of this kind of study is the investigation of the vocabulary size of Shakespeare's works. A count of the different word forms (word types) used by Shakespeare produces an estimate of over 20,000 words (Craig, 2011). This kind of counting treats alternative spellings of the same words as different words, and also considers inflected forms such as *leg* and *legs* as different words.

The biggest problem with such counts is that the words that a person actually uses do not necessarily include all the words that the person knows and could use. Also, the estimated number will depend on how much text is counted. The greater the amount of text counted, the larger the number of different words. At best, such counts give minimum figures. That is, we can say that a person knows at least this number of words.

The productive total vocabulary size of young children

In the early 20th century, several studies were published on the words produced by children. Typically the words were recorded by their parents (Alexander & Chamberlain, 1904; Bohn, 1914; Brandenburg, 1914; Brandenburg & Brandenburg, 1919; Bush, 1914; Gale & Gale, 1902; Heilig, 1913; Langenbeck, 1914; Mateer, 1908; Pelsma, 1914; Rowe & Rowe, 1913; Whipple & Whipple, 1909). Some of these were published in a journal with the impressive title of *The Pedagogical Seminary*. The children were typically part of single-child families where at least one of the parents was an academic. Mateer (1908) is an interesting exception where the data gatherer was a clearly devoted older sister doing her graduate study using data gathered from her four-year-old brother.

The studies were longitudinal and the data was usually gathered over a period of at least ten weeks (following Whipple and Whipple's (1909) example) with some intensive full-day data gathering sessions, although a few studies attempted to record all production over many months.

Many of these studies listed all the different words recorded. The unit of counting was usually the word type but with singular and plural forms being counted as the same item. Also, most of the studies were with children under the age of five, largely because the speed and amount of production by older native-speaker children was just too great to keep pace with, and children went off to school at five where they could not be observed by the parents. The Uhrbrock (1935) study is interesting because it used the new technology of a dictating machine, resulting in the recording of around 24,000 tokens (total running words) on 17 wax cylinders.

There are some interesting lessons to learn from the early productive size studies. As noted above, the length of the data gathering period affected the number of different words recorded. The longer the data gathering period, the more different words were recorded, or to put it another way, the number of tokens recorded directly affects the number of types recorded – a lesson unfortunately not noted by Hart and Risley (1995) in their much later study. It is clear that even a ten-week-long intensive study is not long enough to gather all the words that a child is capable of producing, and a single day of intensive gathering does not get near the number of different words that can be gathered over much longer periods.

These early studies show that young native-speakers' vocabulary knowledge grows very quickly, soon outstripping the ability of a human recorder to keep pace with the new words that are produced. From around the age of two, a native-speaking child increases their productive vocabulary by around 100 words a month (Heilig, 1913), with the more long-term studies showing a two-year-old can produce somewhere around 600–900 different words, a three-year-old around 2000 words (Whipple & Whipple, 1909; Bush, 1914; Brandenburg, 1914), and a four-year-old close to 4000 different words (Brandenburg & Brandenburg, 1919; Langenbeck, 1914). They also show both a variety across different children in the early words that are produced, indicating the important role of particular experience and opportunity in vocabulary growth, as well as a common core of everyday words required for the typical needs of early life.

There are several problems with such studies of productive use, the most critical being that we do not say everything we know, and so such counts are likely to be underestimates. Nonetheless, the results show that very young children know a lot of words and quickly increase their vocabulary sizes, so quickly in fact that such studies became unmanageable without the assistance of recording devices because of children's speedy growth in vocabulary knowledge.

In spite of its long history, the measurement of productive vocabulary size is still a largely unknown field of study. More recent attempts, as in the Hart and Risley (1995) study, have been even more methodologically flawed than the early productive size studies (see Nation & Webb, 2011, 197–201 for a critique). It seems apparent that without gathering very large amounts of output data, we are unlikely to get close to knowing how many words a young native-speaker is capable of producing. The message of the very early studies, however, is that young native-speakers have vocabulary sizes measured in thousands of words, not in tens or hundreds.

Can spoken output be used to measure vocabulary knowledge?

Several studies of young native-speakers of English record their spoken output in a home environment, typically interacting with a parent, and then transcribe and analyse the output to count the different words the child uses and then use the number of different words produced as a measure of their vocabulary knowledge (Hart & Risley, 1995; Hoff, 2003; Hoff & Naigles, 2002; Huttenlocher, Haight, Bryk, Seltzer, & Lyons, 1991; Pan, Rowe, Singer, & Snow, 2005; Rowe, 2012; Rowe, Raudenbush, & Goldin-Meadow, 2012). In some studies, regular collections of output are made and the cumulative number of different words is used as a measure of the child's vocabulary growth. Learners, usually from different socio-economic backgrounds, are compared with each other to see the differences in their vocabulary growth and to suggest causal factors, such as the amount of mother's input, for any difference.

The major methodological question with such studies is whether counting the number of words in a child's output can be used as a reliable and valid measure of vocabulary knowledge, particularly for comparisons between children and at different times in a child's development. The short answer to the question for current studies is clearly no. The reason for this negative answer is that there are several very important factors that affect the number of different words in a child's output of which vocabulary size is only one and not necessarily the most influential. The factors mentioned below are ranked according to our estimation of the likely strength of their influence on the resulting number of types.

The most influential factor affecting the number of different words produced is the number of different tokens produced (Richards & Malvern, 1997). As the number of different tokens increases, the number of different types will also increase. If we want to compare learners on the number of different types they produce, we need to control for the number of tokens produced. That is, we need to have equally sized token samples (samples of the same number of running words). If the samples are of different lengths, then the longer samples are highly likely to contain more different words than the shorter samples. If we do not control for sample length, then primarily we are comparing the effects of different sample lengths not different vocabulary sizes. This failure to control for sample length is a feature of most studies using output as their data gathering tool. The strength of the effect of this factor will depend on the size of the difference in number of tokens in the different samples.

Controlling the amount of time used to collect a spoken sample does not control for the number of tokens produced. Rowe, Raudenbush, and Goldin-Meadow (2012) for example used 90-minute data-gathering sessions. When examining the amount of output children produce (the number of tokens), having a fixed data-gathering time limit is a necessary control. Such a control is not useful when counting the number of types. Having the same number of tokens is the necessary control.

Studies which do not control for the number of tokens are not comparing vocabulary size but are in fact comparing amount of output. Amount of output is useful information and may have some effect on vocabulary development. The unit of counting however for amount of output should not be word types but should be tokens. As described below, there are several other factors affecting the number of word types, and so word types is not a reliable or valid measure of amount of output.

The second most influential factor affecting the number of types produced is the variety of different topics covered. The more varied the topics, the greater the number of types produced, even when the number of tokens is the same (Sutarsyah, Nation, & Kennedy, 1994; Quero, 2015). The effect of a variety of topics can be very strong, even doubling the number of different words in the same number of tokens. In naturalistic studies, it is very difficult to control for diversity of topic, but such diversity strongly affects the nature of the output.

The third most influential factor is the quality of the interaction with the care-giver when the language data is gathered. The more the care-giver supports the child's participation, the richer the vocabulary used by the child is likely to be.

Beyond a fairly minimal level of language proficiency, the fourth most influential factor affecting the number of types produced is the number of words a child knows and is able to produce, that is, their productive vocabulary size.

The fifth most influential factor, the data-gathering situation, is a little indirect. If the data-gathering situation is somewhat intimidating, then the child may be reluctant to speak (Labov, 1973). This reduces the amount of speaking (the number of tokens produced) and thus the number of types produced. It is likely that the skill of the data-gatherers and the rapport they gain with the families involved reduces the effect of this factor. Socio-economic differences may affect this factor.

The sixth most influential factor is what is counted as a word. The three major units of word counting are the token, the word type and the word family (Nation, 2016). If a word is counted every time it appears regardless of whether it has been counted before, then the unit of counting is the token. When we count how long a sample of language use is, we are counting tokens. If we count how many words someone speaks per minute, we are counting tokens. The second sentence of this paragraph contains nineteen tokens. Tokens are sometimes called running words.

Types are different words. The second sentence of the preceding paragraph contains fourteen types. *The* is counted just as one type even though it occurs four times in the sentence. *Word* is counted as one type even though it occurs three times in the sentence. *A* and *an* would be counted as two different types. *Word* and *words* would be counted as two different types. There are several decisions that need to be made when counting word types, such as whether to count hesitations such as *um* and *er*, or just to ignore them, or whether numbers, for example 2016, are counted as words (Nation, 2016).

Some researchers feel that counting *word* and *words* as two different words is inflating a count of vocabulary knowledge. Rowe, Raudenbush, and Goldin-Meadow (2012) preferred to count inflected forms with the same stem as members of the same word family. This particular kind of word family which includes the stem and inflected forms is called a lemma. The strict definition of a lemma separates part of speech. So *walk* and its verbal inflections (*walks, walked, walking*) would be counted as one lemma and *walk* as a noun and its plural form (*walks*) would be counted as a different lemma. Bauer and Nation (1993) describe several levels of word family with the more inclusive levels including both inflected and derived forms. The word family for *work* could include *work, works, worked, working, worker, workers* along with other forms such as *rework* and *unworkable*. For very young children, it seems reasonable to use the type or the lemma as the unit of counting, but as a child's knowledge of the word building devices of English increases, the size of the unit of counting should also increase.

When counting, it is important to clearly describe what the unit of counting is. Different units of counting result in different numbers of words. Most studies do this adequately but their descriptions of the unit of counting could be improved, for example, making it clear whether different parts of speech are included in the same lemma and whether variant forms of the same word, *biscuit* and *bikky* (an informal word for *biscuit*) for example, are counted in the same lemma.

The ranking of the six factors is not absolute but depends on how each factor is dealt with in a particular study. The point of the ranking is to stress that counting the number of different words in a piece of output is a very contaminated measure of vocabulary size. There are many important factors besides vocabulary size that strongly influence the result, and these factors are so influential that they invalidate such counting as a measure of size. Some factors, such as the number of tokens, the data-gathering situation, and the unit of counting, could be controlled for. Others such as variety of topics are much more difficult to control.

Is the cumulative number of types a good way to measure vocabulary growth?

Some studies gather output data from children at various times. They analyse the number of different words in the initial sample and then count the new different words that appear in the next sample (those words that did not appear in the previous sample) as evidence of vocabulary growth (Hart & Risley, 1995). This continues with new words being cumulatively added to the measure from each new sample from the same child. Is this a valid way of measuring vocabulary growth? Let us put aside the argument that was advanced in the previous section that even a one-off output measure is not likely to be valid and assume that counting the types in output is acceptable. A cumulative method of counting will always show an increase. Taking another sample of output and adding it to the previous samples or samples will increase the number of tokens and thus increase the number of types. This will occur if you add the samples in chronological order from the earliest sample to the latest, and even if you put the samples in reverse chronological order. That is, you take the sample when the child is the oldest and list the types. Then you take the sample when they were a bit younger and list the new types, and then take the next previous sample and so on. You can then show that the child's vocabulary grew from when they were, say, four-years-old until when they were two, which is absurd. Using the same methodology, you could show that even samples of output all taken at roughly the same time from the same child show evidence of vocabulary growth if they are analysed cumulatively. Each sample is likely to contain vocabulary that was not in other samples because cumulatively more tokens have been produced, new topics will be covered, and in the case of chronological sequencing, more vocabulary is known.

The basic question is this: Are the words counted as new in each piece of output truly new words that have been acquired since the last gathering session? If they are, then this is evidence of vocabulary growth. If they were known at the last gathering session but not used, then this is not evidence of vocabulary growth but simply evidence of opportunity to show what was known. This opportunity arises through the chance to produce more and different output, through additional tokens and different topics.

The problem with cumulative data analysis comes from exactly the same major factors that affect analysing a single sample of output – not controlling for the number of tokens, and not controlling for topic variation. Any procedure that keeps increasing the number of tokens and does cumulative analysis will show an increase in the number of types.

Is it possible to do data-gathering of a child's output at various intervals to show vocabulary growth?

It is reasonably straightforward to control for the number of tokens so that equally-sized samples of output are being compared. Care needs to be taken in deciding what is counted as a token and in applying such decisions consistently. Any word-counting program would need to be carefully checked to see what criteria the program was using, for example are numbers written as words (e.g. *fourteen, forty-one*) counted differently from those transcribed as numerals (*14, 41*). Are compound words counted as single items or not? Are marginal words such as hesitations (*um, ah*) counted as words?

Controlling topic variation is much more difficult but could be possible by timing data-gathering to coincide with the same kinds of activities such as reading a book together (it would need to be the same book each time or a very similar book), or playing the same game. Unfortunately, there would be familiarity effects and order effects from such repetition.

The major concern is that "new" words appearing in output might not be words which were acquired since the last data-gathering session but are words that were known previous to then but which did not happen to be used. Data-gathering sessions would need to be very long indeed to allow learners to produce every word they could produce. If estimates of young children's total vocabulary sizes are correct (Biemiller, 2005), then children aged 36 months are likely to know several hundred and possibly a few thousand different words.

At the very least, using output to show vocabulary growth would need to use samples of equal numbers of tokens, and would need to be controlled for topic. They would also need to involve large numbers of tokens in each sample to ensure that a child had a chance to show what vocabulary they know. Even then, we could not be certain that the new words in the later samples were truly newly acquired.

Unless the methodology of data-gathering from child output samples is greatly improved, such data gathering is not a valid way of measuring vocabulary growth. Such data-gathering could be used to show changes in the amount of language produced (tokens) or amount of input, but we cannot equate amount of output with vocabulary size. The number of tokens produced could be used as a measure to predict later vocabulary size, but it needs to be called what it is, that is, not a measure of vocabulary growth but a measure of the number of tokens produced.

Critiques of particular studies

Let us now look critically at some of the studies using the number of word types as a measure. It is important to note that the following critiques are questioning part of the methodology of the selected studies, namely the measurement of vocabulary growth using the number of word types produced. The conclusions that the studies reach about the role of socio-economic status and various intervening variables on vocabulary growth may in fact be true. However, because of the weaknesses in the methodology, these studies cannot be said to have showed that.

The word type measure has been used in two ways. One way is to add new types produced at different times to a cumulative list of types to show vocabulary growth (Hart & Risley, 1995). Another way is to compare the total number of types produced at different times to show differences in vocabulary size (Huttenlocher, Haight, Bryk, Seltzer, & Lyons, 1991; Hoff, 2003).

Hart and Risley

Hart and Risley wanted to show that the amount of input the children received affected their vocabulary size. The children's vocabulary size was measured by taking the average of the number of different words in four one-hour observations that each child produced at the ages of 33 to 36 months old. Unfortunately, as we have seen, this is not a measure of vocabulary size or growth. When Hart and Risley measured the number of different words the children produced at this age, they did not control for the number of running words (tokens) that the children produced. The number of different words produced is directly dependent on the number of tokens produced. The more tokens someone produces, the more different words they produce. So, when comparing the number of different words produced, it is essential that the comparisons are based on exactly the same number of tokens. Because Hart and Risley did not control for the number of tokens, they were comparing largely the effect of the number of tokens produced, not the children's vocabulary size.

The new different words produced by each child in each one-hour session were added to a cumulative list for each child which according to Hart and Risley indicated the developmental trajectory of their vocabulary growth (p. 234).

It is not clear if the measure at 34–36 months of age was a count of all the types produced in the four sessions ("We measured vocabulary use as the number of different words a child used per hour averaged at 34–36 months of age." p. 143), or was the last part of the cumulative measure of vocabulary which would only involve new types produced. Whatever the measure was, by not controlling for the number of tokens, Hart and Risley were not measuring vocabulary growth. Surprisingly, Hart and Risley were aware of the problem: "The number of different words a child uses indicates simultaneously how much the child is talking, how varied are the topics and contexts of talk, and the size of the vocabulary from which the child can draw." (p. 143).

The assumption behind using new types as a measure of vocabulary growth is that the new words produced in each one-hour session represent vocabulary learned since the previous monthly one-hour session. As Hart and Risley note, there are many other more likely factors, namely the additional chance to speak (another one-hour session) provides the opportunity for further previously known words to occur. If new topics occur in that session, then this provides further opportunity for both previously known and newly learned words to occur.

Huttenlocher, Haight, Bryk, Seltzer, and Lyons

Huttenlocher, Haight, Bryk, Seltzer, and Lyons (1991) examined the role of parental input in vocabulary growth. They gave careful attention to describing what would be counted as words and the unit of counting (the lemma). They were also keenly aware of the difficulty in using a sample of output to estimate vocabulary size. Their description of how they calculated the words used is not detailed enough. They used the type/token ratio which is very much affected by the number of tokens (Richards & Malvern, 1997), but it seems they controlled for the number of tokens, "we calculated the type/token ratio and used as the base the number of tokens produced by the least talkative child" (p. 240). If this means that the same number of tokens was used to calculate the type/token ratio (which is our interpretation of what they did), then this is good. If the type/token ratios were calculated using different numbers of tokens either within a session or in different sessions, then the ratios cannot be sensibly compared. The same number of tokens would need to be used for every observation in the whole study, not just for those on the same data-gathering occasion, and it is not clear that this was done.

Each of several data-gathering sessions was five hours long for one set of eleven children and three hours for the other eleven. The children were involved in typical daily activities during the data gathering. The children were fourteen or sixteen months old when data-gathering began and were 26 months old when it ended. Each child was involved in three to seven sessions.

The Huttenlocher, Haight, Bryk, Seltzer, and Lyons study dealt well with the factors affecting the measurement of vocabulary knowledge. Firstly, the number of tokens may have been controlled for. To be certain of this, we would need to be told that every data-gathering session was analysed using exactly the same number of tokens. Given the increase in the amount of data gathered in each session as the children were older, it seems unlikely that that much of that data would be discarded to keep the number of tokens the same as in the earliest session. Secondly, although variety of topic was not controlled for, each data-gathering session was several hours long for each child, and the children were at the beginning stages of acquiring a productive vocabulary and thus had small vocabulary sizes. It is likely that the data gathered contained a lot of the vocabulary that the child could produce. Thirdly, the data-gathering procedure tried to be as unobtrusive as possible. Fourthly, the description of what was counted as a word and the unit of counting was clear and detailed.

Vocabulary growth was measured with the assumption that words that appeared in earlier samples were known in later samples. Huttenlocher, Haight, Bryk, Seltzer, and Lyons note that "Although occasionally a word did not reappear in later samples, this was rare, and occurred when the appropriate contexts of use did not continue" (p. 239). This is in effect cumulative counting. We may be uncertain if the occurrence of a word in a later session represented recent learning or the fortunate occurrence of an appropriate context of use for a word known much earlier. Perhaps the substantial time allowed for each data-gathering session at least partially overcame this.

Overall, the Huttenlocher, Haight, Bryk, Seltzer, and Lyons study was very carefully done with attention given to critical factors affecting estimation of vocabulary knowledge. The unknown factor is the use of equally-sized samples of tokens.

Rowe, Raudenbush and Goldin-Meadow

Rowe, Raudenbush and Goldin-Meadow (2012) wanted to measure if the pace of vocabulary growth at 30 months old predicted children's vocabulary skills at 54 months old, just before entry to kindergarten. Vocabulary skill was measured using the Peabody Picture Vocabulary Test (PPVT) (Dunn, 1965). The pace of vocabulary growth was measured using the cumulative number of word types used by the 62 children during nine 90-minute videotaped visits (one every four months) between the ages of 14 and 46 months. "Children's vocabulary growth across the nine sessions from 14 to 46 months was measured as their cumulative word types over time" (p. 512). Word types were used in a formula to model each child's vocabulary growth. Rowe et al. controlled for the amount of time in each session, prorating data based on the number of missing minutes if the session ended a bit sooner than expected to make the data-gathering sessions equal (90 minutes long). Rowe et al. use the term *word type* incorrectly as they actually included inflected forms of the base word as family members, meaning that they probably counted flemmas if they did not distinguish part of speech (Nation, 2016). A *flemma* is a lemma which includes different parts of speech (Nation, 2016). For example, the flemma *talk* includes its verb forms (*talk, talked, talking, talks*), its noun forms (*talk, talks, talking*) and its adjectival uses (*talking*). The mis-use of terminology did not affect their study as they were consistent in how they counted. The number of tokens is not reported but the standard deviations of flemmas were very large, as was the difference between minimum and maximum flemmas.

Rowe et al.'s measure was not a measure of the pace of vocabulary growth. It was primarily a measure of talkativeness, that is, how many tokens were produced, as well as a measure of topic diversity, vocabulary knowledge etc. Perhaps talkativeness is a predictor of vocabulary skill, and perhaps low socio-economic status children's vocabularies grow more slowly, but the measure used in their study cannot be used to show that. Controlling for time is not the same as controlling for the amount of tokens produced, and the critical control is the number of tokens produced. However, even with that control there are other influential factors that make the number of types produced a very poor measure of vocabulary growth.

Hoff

Hoff (2003) recorded interaction between parents and two-year-old children in two sessions 10 weeks apart to measure rates of productive vocabulary development. To some degree, Hoff controlled for the influential variable of topic diversity in each session by recording dressing, mealtime and play interaction where the play involved toys provided by the experimenter. Hoff wisely decided that

> it was considered important not to allow differences among the children in the amount of speech they produced to influence that measure. (This is in contrast to the measure of maternal speech that was designed to capture what children actually heard, not what their mothers could do.) For the children, therefore, equivalent-length speech samples were created by truncating the mealtime, dressing, and toy play transcripts so that each setting contributed in approximately equivalent proportions to the speech sample for each child but so that there were exactly 90 utterances in each speech sample; 90 was the number of utterances available in the smallest speech sample. The measure of productive vocabulary was then the number of word types in the 90-utterance speech sample. (p. 1370)

The problem with Hoff's measure was that controlling for the number of utterances did not control for the number of tokens because the utterances were of differing token lengths. The token lengths of the children's utterances are not reported. Hoff notes that the number of tokens and the number of types in the mothers' speech were highly related, so highly in fact that the number of tokens was dropped as a measure in mothers' speech "because it was essentially redundant with the number of types" (p. 1372). Looking at the type-token relationship in the children's output would probably have shown the same close relationship, which is one of the major points of this critique. In her discussion, Hoff notes that "the words children use in talking … is not a pure measure of vocabulary knowledge" (p. 1375). We certainly agree with that.

The message of this critique is that counting word types in output is not a measure of vocabulary growth because there are several very influential factors affecting what vocabulary is used in output of which vocabulary growth or size is one and not the most important one. The most influential factor is the number of tokens, but even if this is controlled, there are several other important factors that make the number of types produced a poor measure of vocabulary knowledge and growth.

In Chapter 9 we look at several ways of measuring the vocabulary growth of very young children.

CHAPTER 3

Dictionary-based studies of vocabulary size

In Chapter 2 we looked at output as a way of measuring a child's vocabulary size. In this chapter we look at using dictionaries as a source of words to measure vocabulary size. This approach to measuring vocabulary size led most researchers into very severe methodological errors and resulted in very misleading estimates of vocabulary size.

One of the earliest published investigations of vocabulary size was Holden's (1875) study of the words in a dictionary that he already could use. Kirkpatrick (1891) did a similar self-report study of his knowledge of the words in Webster's unabridged dictionary. Since then, there have been numerous attempts to estimate the vocabulary size of native-speakers using dictionaries as starting points. There is little point in providing a chronological account of the research because, with one or two notable exceptions, researchers were unaware of the relevant previous research. This at best resulted in the rediscovery of the same principles and at worst, and most often, resulted in very misleading estimates of vocabulary size.

The aim of this chapter is to describe the procedures that should be followed when using a dictionary to provide the basis for an estimate of vocabulary size. This will be done by examining the few studies that suggested the procedures and then by listing and describing the procedures. The basic question answered here is "How can we take a representative sample from a dictionary?"

Group administered measures of vocabulary size have involved taking a random sample of words from a dictionary, usually by taking the first or nth word on every nth page. This random sample is a proportion of the dictionary. In the Goulden, Nation, & Read (1990) study, the sample was a one in five-hundred sample of the headwords in the dictionary. A person's score on a test based on the sample is multiplied by the proportion (500 times in the Goulden et al study) to gain an estimate of total receptive vocabulary size.

Thorndike's review (1924)

The earliest and most important study in this area that gave careful consideration to the methodology is "The vocabularies of school pupils" by Edward Thorndike (1924). Because this paper is difficult to access, it has been included as Appendix 3 in this book. Thorndike reviewed nine studies of vocabulary size, finding a wide difference in their estimates. He argued that this disparity was largely the result of the effect of the sampling method used, combined with dictionary size. In his review he described four procedures that should have guided subsequent research but which were not always followed by later researchers. Firstly, he showed the importance of using a sample source, a dictionary or frequency list, that did not exclude words likely to be known by the people being investigated. Any vocabulary study that used a sample source that was too small would underestimate vocabulary size.

Secondly, Thorndike showed that it was necessary to have clearly stated criteria regarding what was to be included in a word family. For Thorndike, those criteria were the same as those to be used for the Thorndike and Lorge (1944) word frequency list. Thus, most words with derivational suffixes were considered to be different words from the base form and other derived forms. As we shall see, failing to include derived forms in a word family will bias the sampling towards better known items. Most critical, however, was the decision regarding subsequent homographs. Many words, particularly high frequency words, have several entries in the dictionary. *Draw* has two entries in Webster's 3rd Dictionary, one for the verb uses and one for the noun uses. Because there are several entries there is more likelihood of such forms being chosen in the sampling.

Any dictionary-based vocabulary size study that did not have well thought out criteria would be leaving the decisions to the dictionary makers. This would usually result in an overestimation of vocabulary size.

Thirdly, and most importantly, Thorndike demonstrated that it was necessary to use a sampling procedure that did not bias the selection towards high frequency words. Procedures that involved choosing the first word on a page regardless of whether it was the first full entry and whether it was a subsequent homograph were particularly susceptible to this bias. This bias occurred simply because high frequency words occupied more space per entry and had relatively more entries than low frequency words. The greater the size of the dictionary, the more the space given to high frequency words, and thus the greater the overestimation of vocabulary size. Thorndike suggested two ways of overcoming this bias. One way was to number all the entries and select every nth word. "To take a random sample of 100 words from a dictionary containing, say, 28,000, we should take words 1, 281, 561, 841 etc., or words 2, 282, 562, 842 etc., or the equivalent" (p. 73). Another way is to select the first word whose definition *begins* on that page, as long as subsequent homographs are allowed for (Thorndike, 1924, footnote 1, p. 73). Unfortunately, this way could introduce bias because of the higher selection probability for words on pages containing few words. Such a procedure is a one stage cluster sampling with one item (a word) sampled per cluster (a page). In order to avoid bias, clusters need to be the same size. Studies that use procedures that introduce bias will greatly overestimate vocabulary size because their samples will contain too many high frequency words which will be known by most people sitting the tests.

Fourthly, Thorndike demonstrated a way of checking the representativeness of the sample. He used the 1921 edition of *The Teacher's Word Book* (Thorndike, 1921a), a word frequency list, to see if the samples used in Gerlach's (1917) and Brandenburg's (1918) studies contained an appropriate number of words from the various frequency levels. He found that both samples were heavily biased towards high frequency words.

Thorndike found that none of the nine studies published between 1907 and 1919 that he reviewed was methodologically sound. They failed on three and sometimes on all four of the procedures he suggested.

These four procedures were sufficient to provide representative samples for vocabulary size research, but unfortunately Thorndike's review was published in a collection of papers rather than in a more easily accessible journal. Indeed, the first reference to this 1924 review is in a 1953 study by Bryan which refers to the review but fails to make use of its findings. The second reference to the review is in a 1963 review by Lorge and Chall. Lorge was a student and colleague of Thorndike and the review made use of Thorndike's suggestions.

Later reviews (1930s to 1960s)

After Thorndike, the next article to address the methodology of the measurement of vocabulary size sensibly was Williams (1932). Williams compared a sample drawn from a dictionary with an independent list of children's vocabulary. He found that the number of words from the children's list in the dictionary sample was much greater (by 4.5 times) than it should be. Apparently, Williams was not aware of Thorndike's review. However, he reached the same conclusion that the spaced sampling method combined with dictionary size resulted in an overabundance of high frequency words in the sample. The two sampling procedures he described to overcome this bias were the same as those described by Thorndike eight years earlier. Williams also pointed out that using abridged dictionaries could result in an underestimation of technical or specialist vocabularies. Williams thus rediscovered three of the four procedures described by Thorndike.

Lorge and Chall (1963) in a critical analysis of the widely described Seashore and Eckerson (1940) study elaborated on the remaining procedure of setting up clearly described criteria for deciding what was to be counted as a word. They argued that proper names, geographical place names, word parts, and names of flora and fauna should be excluded from measures of vocabulary size. They found that the Seashore and Eckerson test greatly overestimated vocabulary size because it did not apply three of the four procedures suggested by Thorndike. Seashore and Eckerson did not set up sufficient criteria for what was to be counted, but relied on the dictionary makers' decisions. They did not use a suitable sampling procedure and did not use an external check on the representativeness of their sample. Words with multiple entries were a particular influential source of bias towards high frequency items in their sample. Seashore and Eckerson were aware of Williams's (1932) study but failed to see its significance for their study.

Seashore and Eckerson however did make use of an internal reliability check on their sampling which was a useful addition to the four procedures described by Thorndike. Seashore and Eckerson compared proportions of parts of speech in sub-samples to see if they were similar.

Unfortunately, the most perceptive critics of attempts at making dictionary-based tests did not make their own and it has been left to others to put their suggested procedures into practice. It is sufficient to say that none of the twenty or more published studies of vocabulary size since 1907 has made full use of the necessary procedures. They have thus produced misleading estimates.

There has been a revival of interest in vocabulary size and knowledge, partly as a result of argument over the feasibility and effectiveness of direct vocabulary teaching. This interest has led to research which allows us to build on the procedures described by Thorndike, and the rest of this chapter draws on this research to restate, add to and refine the sampling procedures that a proper dictionary based study of vocabulary size must follow.

Procedures for drawing a representative sample from a dictionary

1. Choose a dictionary that is big enough to cover the known vocabulary of the people being investigated.

This does not necessarily mean that an unabridged dictionary must be used when studying the vocabulary size of educated adult native-speakers. Recalculations of methodologically faulty studies (Thorndike, 1924; Lorge & Chall, 1963) and data from recent more methodologically sound studies (Goulden, Nation, & Read, 1990; D'Anna, Zechmeister, & Hall, 1991) indicate that educated adult native-speakers' base word vocabulary is around twenty thousand words. So, for educated adults a dictionary should contain at least 30,000 base words. This is easily within the range of abridged desktop dictionaries such as *Collins English Dictionary*. D'Anna, Zechmeister, and Hall (1991) checked the inclusiveness of the *Oxford American Dictionary* by comparing it with two advanced word lists. Goulden, Nation, and Read (1990) supplemented Webster's 3rd by using recent addenda.

2. Use a reliable way of discovering the total number of entries in the dictionary.

In order to make calculations of vocabulary size it is necessary to know the total number of entries in the dictionary, or the total number of the particular types of words, such as base words, that are the focus of the study. Dictionary makers are not greatly concerned about the number of entries in a dictionary except to the extent that this can be used to advertise the dictionary and increase its sales. Not surprisingly, publishers' statements exaggerate the number of entries. For example, Webster's 3rd claims to have 450,000 entries. Two independent studies (Dupuy, 1974; Goulden, Nation, & Read, 1990) reach the same figure of 267,000. *The Shorter Oxford English Dictionary* in a computer based count was found to have 73,582 entries (Dolby & Resnikoff, 1967). The note on the dust-jacket however says 163,000.

Diller (1978) accepted the Webster's 3rd figure of 450,000 without checking and, because the number of words in the testing sample in proportion to the total number of entries was the basis for his calculations, reached wildly inflated estimates of vocabulary size.

The total number of entries can be found by counting each entry manually (D'Anna, Zechmeister, & Hall, 1991) or with a computer, or by counting a sample of the dictionary (Dupuy, 1974; Goulden, Nation, & Read, 1990).

3. Use explicit criteria for deciding and stating (a) what items will not be included in the count and (b) what will be regarded as members of a word family.

The main reason for excluding items from a sample or an estimation of dictionary size is to avoid the effect that the dictionary makers' inclusion policies can have on the estimation of vocabulary size.

Lorge and Chall (1963) consider it "debatable" (p. 149) and "highly questionable whether [encyclopedic and word part entries] can be considered 'words' for estimating vocabulary knowledge" (p. 151). Encyclopedic entries include names of historical personages, fictional characters, geographical place names, and the scientific names of flora and fauna. As well as it being questionable whether to include these as words, the major difficulty lies in the arbitrary nature of their inclusion in the dictionary. If geographical place names are included for example, where does the inclusion stop? Will the name of *every* country in the world be included or only those thought to be of interest in areas where the dictionary is sold? If plant and animal names are included, what about the multitude of insects and bacteria? Dictionaries clearly differ on their policies of what will be included and this is not usually stated in a rigorous way.

By excluding types of words where different dictionary makers have different policies and by limiting the estimation of vocabulary size to the types of words that all would agree on as a part of someone's vocabulary, it is possible to make an estimation of vocabulary size that can be generalized beyond the particular dictionary studied. This estimation can then be used for more than relative purposes and can be used as a tool for research into the relationship between vocabulary size, skill in language use, and the acquisition of knowledge.

Another important reason for excluding items from the count is practicality. When estimating vocabulary size, the smaller the ratio of the sample to the whole dictionary, the more sensitive the measurement will be. For example, a sample which is one-twentieth of the dictionary is better than a sample which is one-hundredth of the same dictionary. However, the smaller the ratio, the greater the number of words in the sample, and the greater the difficulty of testing them all in a reasonable time. It is thus more practical to reduce the size of the dictionary by excluding items. For example, the exclusion of proper names, compound words, and various items like abbreviations, word parts, symbols etc. from a study of Webster's 3rd reduced the total size by almost 50% (Goulden et al., 1990).

Another reason for having criteria for inclusion is to avoid a bias in sampling towards high frequency words. There is a reasonably strong connection between frequency of occurrence in the language and likelihood of people knowing the word (Anderson & Freebody, 1983). It is important that words with related forms and meanings are dealt with as word families. This means that either all items except the base form are excluded from the sampling or that the related forms are sampled separately from the base form and are tested in a different part of the test. If this is not done, then the sampling will be biased towards high frequency items because high frequency items have more related forms than low frequency items. Clearly, regarding items such as *legal, legalese, legalism, legality, legalize,* which are all separate entries in the *Collins English Dictionary*, as different words would increase size estimates. Different dictionary makers have different policies regarding related forms. Some list them under the base word, but list homographs with a related meaning but a different part of speech separately. Others list related forms as separate entries. Dictionary makers also differ in whether they include compound words which are made up of items that are already included in the dictionary with similar meanings, such as *dishwasher*.

Thorndike (1924) regarded a word family as consisting of the base form, and the base plus *-s, -ed, -ing, -er, -est* and *-ly*. Research (Tyler & Nagy, 1989; White, Power, & White, 1989) shows that particularly with children aged ten and above it is reasonable to assume that they are able to derive the meanings of words with common prefixes and suffixes and a known related base form. There are frequency studies of prefixes (Stauffer, 1942; Bock, 1948) which can help in setting up criteria for dealing with such items. Here are examples of derived forms from *Collins English Dictionary* that have a clear meaning relationship to their base form and are all separate entries. *Unreal, premarital, transatlantic, misbelief, cranial, craniate* (having a skull or cranium), *craniology* (branch of science concerned with the shape of the skull), *craniometer, craniometry*, and *craniotomy*.

Goulden, Nation, and Read (1990) used the following criteria for classifying items as derived words.

> A corresponding base word must occur as a main entry in the dictionary. The meaning of the derived word must be clear from the meaning of the parts that make up the word or involve the minimum of extra learning... Words consisting of common prefixes... attached to base words are marked "derived". (p. 345)

Nagy and Anderson's (1984) scale was used to determine degree of relatedness and provide a cut-off point.

It is also necessary to have criteria for deciding consistently which form will be considered as the base form. Usually it should be the least inflected form but sometimes a form with an affix is much more frequent (*computer* is much more frequent than *compute*). When two or more forms such as *jurisprudence* and *jurisprudent* are the least inflected forms, then either part of speech, order of occurrence in the dictionary, form of the definition (does the definition of one contain the other form?), frequency, or historical criteria must be used to make a decision. The criteria for doing this should be clearly described.

Thorndike (1924), Williams (1932) and Lorge and Chall (1963) showed the importance of treating subsequent homographs of a word separately. The failure to have criteria for dealing with these items was a major cause of overestimation of vocabulary size in most studies. As we shall see in the next section, subsequent homographs of related meaning to the first entry must be excluded from the sampling.

A properly conducted sampling can take account of the various types of words in the dictionary. There is no need to have to keep to the policies of exclusion used by other researchers as long as the sampling criteria are clearly stated with examples, and figures are given for the various types. This allows other researchers to make calculations and adjustments according to their own policy.

4. Use a sampling procedure that is not biased towards items which occupy more space and have more entries.

When sampling, the criteria for exclusion and inclusion of items can be applied before, while or after the sampling is done depending on practicality.

Thorndike (1924) suggested using numbered entries. This means counting off every nth word and including it in the sample. Subsequent homographs and derived forms would need to be distinguished.

Thorndike (1924) also indicated that choosing the nth complete entry which was not a subsequent homograph on every nth page was an alternative procedure. This procedure was used by Goulden, Nation and Read (1990), but it has problems if simple random sampling is assumed because each page contains a different number of words and pages with a few words are overweighted in estimates of vocabulary size. Pages with a few words tend to contain high frequency words.

Another approach is to use a random sampling technique. *The English Word Speculum* (Dolby & Resnikoff, 1967) contains a randomized list of all the main entries in *The Shorter Oxford English Dictionary* with homographs removed.

D'Anna, Zechmeister, & Hall (1991) used a stratified sampling technique based on the letters of the alphabet. This type of sampling helps overcome bias by making the structure of the sample represent as closely as possible the structure of the population by having the same proportion of words beginning with each letter in the sample as in the population.

The goal of all these procedures is to end up with a representative, non-biased sample of a manageable size.

5. Choose a sample that is large enough to allow an estimate of vocabulary size that can be given with a reasonable degree of confidence.

Surprisingly, the absolute size of a sample has a greater effect on the accuracy of estimates than the proportion of the population sampled, particularly in the case of dictionary sampling where the sample size is not close to the size of the total dictionary. If we want to be sure that the true value of an individual learner's score on a test using the sample lies close to the learner's observed score, we need to have a large enough sample. Table 3.1 uses calculations based on the normal approximation to a binomial distribution to show the effect of sample size on the maximum range of true values on either side of the observed score.

Table 3.1 Confidence intervals at the 90% level for different sample sizes for simple random sampling

Number of items in the sample	Maximum confidence interval*
100	+/– 8%
150	+/– 7%
200	+/– 6%
300	+/– 5%
400	+/– 4%
600	+/– 3%
1200	+/– 2%

* We can be 90% sure that the true value of the score lies within +/– this percentage of the observed score

Table 3.1 shows that if the sample size was 100 words, then we are reasonably confident that the true value of an individual learner's observed score would lie anywhere within a sixteen per cent range. Thus, if the learner's observed score on the test was 50 out of 100 (50%), we could be 90% sure that the true value of her score lay between 42 (42%) and 58 (58%) out of 100 (i.e. a range of plus and minus 8%). However, if a sample of 600 items was used and a learner scored 300 out of 600 (50%), we could be 90% sure that the true value of the learner's score lay somewhere between 282 (47%) and 318 (53%) (i.e. a range of +/– 3%). Note that although the range in number of items is larger, the percentage is smaller, and the percentage is used when estimating from a sample to the whole dictionary. According to the values in Table 3.1, to usefully narrow the range of the true value further, the sample size would have to be increased to 1200 items. This is too large for a manageable test of vocabulary size.

The size of the maximum confidence interval has an important effect on the usefulness of a vocabulary size test. *Collins English Dictionary*, a medium sized dictionary, contains 31,100 base words. A 1 in 50 sample of this dictionary would contain 622 items. A test using this number of items would have a confidence interval of +/–3%. This is a 6% range which represents 1,866 items in the 31,100 pool. The best information available suggests that the vocabulary size of native-speakers of English grows by about 1,000 base words a year. A test containing 622 items could not be used to confidently measure yearly and possibly two yearly increases in an individual's vocabulary size because the amount of increase would be within the range of the confidence interval.

In order to test this number of items within a feasible length of time it would be necessary to use test items that could be responded to very quickly, to make the test computer-adaptive perhaps using coarse and fine measures (Meara & Jones, 1987), and to order the test words according to their frequency of occurrence in the language so that sections of them could be assumed to be known and need not be tested.

With group measures of vocabulary size different calculations involving ANOVA, possibly non-parametric, are required and the word sample sizes for each individual could be much smaller. The word sample size, the subject sample size (people sitting the test), and the range of variability in the scores would have to interact to produce a maximum confidence interval of +/–.5% for the proportion of the dictionary known. This is because a dictionary needs to contain at least 30,000 words (Step 1). As probable yearly increases could range from 300 to 1,000 words, a one in fifty sample (600 items) with a confidence level of +/–.5% would be needed to measure yearly increases. This means that a learner's score on the test would probably increase by 6 to 20 items (representing 300 to 1,000 words in the dictionary) and 6 out of 600 is 1% or +/–.5%. In group measures it is better to have a smaller word sample size and a large subject sample size than a larger word sample size and fewer subjects. The greater the range of variability in the test scores, the greater the number of subjects needed to sit the test. Sample sizes cannot be estimated without knowing the variability of vocabulary size between individuals within groups. To be balanced against this however is the need to have a large enough sample size to provide a ratio of sample to population that is sensitive enough to measure change.

6. The sampling should be checked for the reliability of the application of the criteria for exclusion and inclusion of items.

There are several ways of carrying out such checks, particularly to see if the criteria for deciding what is to be included as words are consistently applied. For example, the sample can be done in sections and the figures for each section compared, or more than one person can do part of the sampling, and an inter-rater reliability check can be carried out. If the decision being made is simply whether an item is a base word or not, then the accuracy of the classification could be checked at the .01 level of significance by the other rater working on a total of 14 items (7 base words and 7 non-base words). A .85 agreement is tolerable for data with two response alternatives (Rosenthal, 1987: 64–67). If there are more than two categories, for example base word, derived word, proper noun, compound word, then fewer items would need to be checked in each category, although the total checked would rise compared to the total for two category checks. With more categories the tolerable level of agreement could be a little less than .85. This internal check is not a substitute for an external check using a frequency list.

7. The sample should be checked against a frequency list to make sure that there is no bias in the sampling towards high frequency items.

If the sampling is properly carried out according to the procedures described in this chapter, then when the sample is compared to the words in a frequency count such as Thorndike and Lorge (1944); Francis and Kucera (1982); Carroll, Davies, and Richman (1971) or the BNC/COCA lists (Nation, 2016), there should be proportionally the appropriate number of words at each frequency level in the sample. For example, if each word in the sample represents 100 words in the dictionary then there should be 10 words in the sample in the 1,000 most frequent words in the frequency list (10 × 100). Similarly, there should be 10 words in the sample from the second 1,000 most frequent words and so on.

This procedure of checking was used by Thorndike (1924); Williams (1932) and Lorge and Chall (1963) and in all cases revealed bias in the studies they checked. Goulden, Nation and Read (1990) did a similar check and found it necessary to recalculate the number of words at the various levels in the Thorndike and Lorge (1944) frequency count to match the definition of a word family used in the sampling from the dictionary. Thorndike and Lorge defined a word family as including the base form and the base form plus the inflectional suffixes *-s, -ed, -ing, -er, -est,* and the derivational suffix-*ly*. Goulden et al included many more items in their definition of what was a word family. So, derived items that were separate entries in the Thorndike and Lorge count, such as *lengthen* and *lengthwise*, were included in the same word family and excluded from the Goulden et al. sample. When this same way of making a word family is applied to the Thorndike and Lorge count, the 30,000 items reduce to 13,900 items with 6,100 in the first 10,000, 3,600 in the second 10,000, and 4,200 in the third 10,000. Once these necessary recalculations were made, Goulden, Nation, and Read (1990) found that their samples were not biased towards high frequency items.

8. In the written report of the study, describe clearly and explicitly how each of the previous seven procedures was followed in sufficient detail to allow replication of any or all of the procedures.

Using the eight procedures described above, it is possible to review studies of vocabulary size and see where faulty methodology led to faulty estimation. Such reviews (Thorndike, 1924; Lorge & Chall, 1963) agree with the very rough rule of thumb that for people up to the age of 18 years we can multiply their age in years minus 2 by 1,000 base words or less per year to get an indication of probable vocabulary size in word families. More importantly, however, the procedures should be used to carry out methodologically sound studies that will provide information that can be relied upon in order to explore the many roles of vocabulary knowledge in intellectual activity.

Examples of the effects of not applying the steps

To conclude this chapter, it is instructive to look at some studies that did not follow the steps described above and to see how not following the steps affected the results.

The Seashore and Eckerson (1940) study was critiqued by Lorge and Chall (1963) considering Thorndike's four criteria which are the same as steps 1, 3, 4 and 7 in Table 3.2. Seashore and Eckerson used Funk and Wagnall's (1937) two volume new standard dictionary of the English language. They considered it large enough for their study. The number of words in the dictionary was checked by analysing twenty-seven equally-spaced pages of the dictionary, counting basic and derivative words separately according to the dictionary's classification, with derivatives being broken down into other parts of speech, compound words, multiple meanings, and variants in spelling. Seashore and Eckerson used the dictionary-makers' definition of a word family and the dictionary-makers' distinction of basic and derived forms. Alternative meanings and alternative spellings were not counted as different basic words. Seashore and Eckerson sampled the third basic word in the first column on every left-hand page, giving an initial list of 1,378 words. The sampling method was the major factor causing the inflated estimates.

Table 3.2 The steps applied to Seashore & Eckerson (1940)

	Steps	Application
1	Choose a large dictionary	Well done. A large recent dictionary was chosen.
2	Carefully estimate the number of words in the dictionary	Moderately well done. Several pages were analysed.
3	Have clear criteria for deciding what is a word and what is included in a word family	Poorly done. The dictionary-makers' categories were accepted and counted.
4	Use a non-biased procedure for sampling	Poorly done. A page-based sampling method was used.
5	Make a large enough sample	Well done. The sample involved well over 1000 words.
6	Check the application of criteria	Poorly done. The dictionary-makers' criteria were not checked.
7	Check the sample for frequency bias	Poorly done. The sample was not checked.
8	Clearly describe the steps and procedures used	Well done. The steps are clear though dependent on the dictionary-makers' criteria.

Seashore and Eckerson (1940) divided their sample into four equivalent sets with around 330 items in each test and tested receptive knowledge using four-item multiple-choice tests. Basic common, basic rare and derived forms were tested separately. College students were estimated to have a vocabulary size of over 58,186 basic common words. Knowledge of rare words and derived forms added 1,662 and 95,888 words to this giving a grand total of 155,736 words.

Lorge and Chall (1963) found that 30% of Seashore and Eckerson's basic words were proper names, (persons and geographical places) and word parts. They also found that many words had multiple entries and these multiple entries, making up 9% of the dictionary's entries, were counted as separate words. When checking Seashore and Eckerson's test sample against the Thorndike and Lorge first 20,000, they found twice as many higher frequency words than there should be. The methodological errors of not sensibly deciding what will be counted as words and a very biased sampling method resulted in gross over-estimates of vocabulary sizes. Several subsequent pieces of research used the same tests, perpetuating the same errors.

In a chapter titled *How long does it take to produce a bilingual?*, Diller (1978) estimated the vocabulary sizes of native-speakers of English. His goal was to see how many years a second language learner would need to study to have the vocabulary size of a native-speaker. Diller wisely chose a large dictionary of American English because he wanted to measure the vocabulary size of a wide range of adults. Unfortunately, Diller believed the advertising on the dictionary instead of doing his own careful estimate. The number of entries in a dictionary is used to "sell" the dictionary and is typically inflated, in the case of Diller's dictionary, 450,000 entries. The more accurate figure is nearer 267,000 words (Dupuy, 1974; Goulden, Nation & Read, 1990), and is likely to be much lower than that if consistent word and word family criteria are applied. Diller simply accepted the dictionary maker's criteria of what is considered a word, taking each entry, even entries of different uses of the same word and multiword units as different words. He seems to have sampled the first word on every left-hand page until he had 1000 words. This sampling procedure heavily biased his sample in favour of high frequency words. The Kucera and Francis (1967) frequency count was available and is mentioned in Diller's chapter, but was not used as a check. Diller's procedure is reasonably clearly described, but there is little to describe as he simply accepted the dictionary-makers' statements and conventions.

Table 3.3 The steps applied to Diller (1978)

	Steps	Application
1	Choose a large dictionary	Well done. Diller chose the largest American dictionary available.
2	Carefully estimate the number of words in the dictionary	Poorly done. Diller accepted the dictionary-makers' figure of 450,000 entries
3	Have clear criteria for deciding what is a word and what is included in a word family	Poorly done. Diller accepted each entry as a word.
4	Use a non-biased procedure for sampling	Poorly done. Diller took the upper left-hand words on left -hand pages.
5	Make a large enough sample	Well done. Diller chose 1000 words.
6	Check the application of criteria	Poorly done. No criteria were applied.
7	Check the sample for frequency bias	Poorly done. The sample was not checked.
8	Clearly describe the steps and procedures used	Moderately well done.

Diller used a Yes/No test which also included an "unsure" category.

> The data suggests that children in grade school learn to recognise more than 10,000 words each year. Then there is a spurt in junior high when they learn 20,000 or 30,000 a year. At about age 16 there is levelling off at 48% of the dictionary, or 216,000 words, as the students approach what seems to be a literate adult vocabulary level. (p. 129)

Diller saw seven-year olds as having a vocabulary of 54,000 words, 10-year olds 112,000 words, 15-year olds 198,000 words, and college professors 247,500 words. He marvelled that junior high school students were increasing their vocabulary "by some 75 words EVERY DAY without any serious effort" (p. 131). These vocabulary size figures are clearly absurd and are the result of very faulty methodology, particularly in estimating how many words the dictionary contained and then in gaining a representative sample of the words in the dictionary. In addition, the failure to clearly define what should be counted as a word inflated the results.

An example of applying the steps

It is possible to use a dictionary to calculate total vocabulary size, but it would require using the dictionary to make a word list and this word list could then be used for sampling to make tests. The construction of the word list would require the use of clear explicit criteria that would be likely to be different from the criteria used to make dictionary entries. Some of the construction could be computerised but the creation of the list would require a lot of human judgement and checking. Let us look at the D'Anna, Zechmeister, & Hall (1991) study that did this.

Table 3.4 The steps applied to D'Anna, Zechmeister, & Hall (1991)

	Steps	**Application**
1	Choose a large dictionary	Well done. D'Anna, Zechmeister, and Hall used the *Oxford American Dictionary* which they checked against two large word lists.
2	Carefully estimate the number of words in the dictionary	Well done. Each word in the dictionary, according to the criteria, was counted and a further sample checked.
3	Have clear criteria for deciding what is a word and what is included in a word family	Well done. A clear list of types of exclusions was made and checked against another dictionary.
4	Use a non-biased procedure for sampling	Probably well done. There was proportional random stratified sampling from each letter of the alphabet.
5	Make a large enough sample	Well done. Two 200 word samples.
6	Check the application of criteria	Well done. Two errors were found later.
7	Check the sample for frequency bias	Not done. The sample was not checked.
8	Clearly describe the steps and procedures used	Very well done.

D'Anna, Zechmeister, and Hall (1991) used tests which included a small number of pseudo-words. The words in the tests were in random order. The tests were like Yes/No tests except that for words said to be known, the degree of knowledge was rated on a four-point scale. Data from test-takers who rated five or more of the nine pseudo-words as known was excluded from the study. For the college students tested, the data from the two samples gave very similar results, indicating they knew 16,785 of the 26,901 words, using the top two points of the rating scale. The students tested ranged in age from 18 to 22-years-old with an average age of 19.6 years. The results follow the rough rule of thumb of age minus 2 times 1000.

This chapter has focused on the methodology of sampling to make tests. In general tests based on sampling from a dictionary have not provided realistic results because of the methodological problems involved. Sampling is just one of several issues in the measurement of vocabulary size. Others, also noted by Thorndike (1924), are "What do we mean when we say someone knows a word?", "What test item types should we use to measure this knowledge?" and "What is the significance of vocabulary size?" These issues need to be considered in systematic and explicit ways drawing on the lessons and results of previous studies.

CHAPTER 4

The receptive vocabulary sizes of young native-speakers of English

The studies in this chapter are involved in measuring the vocabulary sizes of young school children. They use various kinds of measures but share the common feature of sampling from substantial lists of English words rather than dictionaries. The pioneer in this work in developing word lists is Edward Thorndike. Nowadays, the work involved in developing word lists with the help of computers is substantial, but in Thorndike's time without the help of computers the amount of work was enormous, and it is not surprising that there were gaps of ten years or more between the completion of each of his three word lists.

Edward Thorndike

Thorndike was aware of the difficulties involved in using dictionaries to measure vocabulary size (Thorndike, 1924) and developed a cumulative series of word lists based on word frequency and range. The first list contained 10,000 words, published in *The Teacher's Word Book* (1921a), the second list contained 20,000 words (1931), and the final list was *The Teacher's Word Book of 30,000 Words* (Thorndike & Lorge, 1944). The unit of counting was largely the flemma (Thorndike & Lorge, 1944, p. ix). Thorndike described the value of the list as being a way of finding out how common a word is which could then guide decisions about whether to use a word in speaking or writing, or about whether to teach or learn it. It was also clearly of value to researchers such as him in making vocabulary size tests. Dale (1931) criticized the 1931 list for not dealing with homographs and homonyms and for not taking account of word families. Dale also indicated the need to find out how well learners actually knew the words. The choice between frequency and the likelihood of a word being known is a theme that continues to occur in vocabulary size studies. Dale went on to do research on how well learners knew words, resulting in the *Living Word Vocabulary* (Dale & O'Rourke, 1976, 1981), which Biemiller (2005) drew on in his studies of vocabulary size.

Thorndike made a 100 item five-choice multiple-choice test based on the first 20,000 words that is briefly reported on in Thorndike (1924). There he estimates that the average first year high school pupil, presumably around 13 years old, would know from 10,000 to 11,500 words (flemmas including adverbial *-ly*). This figure agrees closely with the Coxhead, Nation and Sim (2015) data described in Chapter 5.

Unfortunately, we cannot find any other published evidence of uses of Thorndike's test with young native-speakers, but given the size and nature of the *Teachers Word Book* lists it seems highly likely that the results of using his test would be similar to those reported by Biemiller (2005) and Biemiller and Slonim (2001).

Biemiller (2005) and Biemiller and Slonim's (2001) studies

Most studies of the receptive vocabulary size of native-speakers of English focus on adults (Goulden, Nation, & Read, 1990; D'Anna, Zechmeister, & Hall, 1991; Coxhead, Nation, & Sim, 2014; Brysbaert, Stevens, Mandera, & Keuleers, 2016), but Biemiller and Slonim (2001) and Biemiller (2005) measured the vocabulary size of children from kindergarten (age 5) to grade 6 (age 12) using a spoken interview test with the younger children and a written recall test of the same format with the older children who could read and write. For the young children, the test involved the researcher reading aloud a sentence to the child, for example *John got his **math** work done quickly* and asking, *What does **math** mean?* Any answer that indicated some knowledge of the word was accepted as correct. Biemiller and Slonim (2001) checked the reliability of this test by comparing different forms of the same test testing different words, by comparing the same words tested in different context sentences, and by comparing multiple-choice and open-ended versions of the test. All correlated above .8. Note that the contexts used in the sentences are not neutral but typically provide small clues to the meaning and contain a common collocate (*Johnny caught a **fish**. He felt a lump in his **throat**. The **flood** caused a lot of damage to the town.*). Biemiller (2005) and Biemiller and Slonim (2001) found a wide range of vocabulary sizes at each age level, and a clearly identifiable sequence of known words determined not by age as much as by vocabulary size. That is, learners progressed through roughly the same order of particular words as their vocabulary size increased. Biemiller and Slonim used Dale and O'Rourke's (1981) book, *The Living Word Vocabulary*, as the source of 17,570 root words for the tests. Biemiller (2010) subsequently published his own list, *Words Worth Teaching*, for teachers, largely because he found that grade level and age level was not as useful a predictor of word knowledge as current vocabulary size.

Biemiller and Slonim found that young native-speakers of English acquire around 800–1000 word families a year, a result that agrees with the early productive studies mentioned in Chapter 2. Table 4.1 roughly summarises and rounds off Biemiller's (2005, p. 233) findings for young native-speakers at school.

Table 4.1 Average native-speaker total vocabulary sizes for various age levels

Age	Average vocabulary size	Range of sizes
5 year olds	3,000 word families	1,000-5,000
6 year olds	4,000 word families	1,500-5,000
7 year olds	5,000 word families	2,000-8,500
8 year olds	6,000 word families	3,000-10,000
9 year olds	7,000 word families	4,000-11,000
10 year olds	8,000 word families	5,500-12,000
11 year olds	9,000 word families	7,000-13,000

It is worth noting that even the lowest scoring native-speakers at most levels knew several thousand words, and that at each age level there was a wide range of vocabulary sizes. The progression follows the rough rule of thumb for vocabulary growth, namely to make a guess at a particular learner's vocabulary size, take their age minus 2 times 1000. So, a seven-year old should know around 5,000 word families ($7-2 \times 1000 = 5000$).

The *Living Word Vocabulary* (Dale & O'Rourke, 1981) involved the testing of 44,000 meanings of words to determine at which grade level each particular word was likely to be known. Although the book was published in 1981, Dale signalled his interest in the work in an article critiquing Thorndike's second word list in 1931.

Dale and O'Rourke used three-choice multiple-choice tests. A word was considered to be known at a particular grade level when 67% to 84% of at least 200 children at a particular grade level answered the item correctly. The word was assigned to the lowest grade level that met the 67% to 84% criterion. The testing was done in even numbered grade levels, testing up to grade 16, and beginning with the fourth grade. The fourth grade was chosen because the test involved reading and the researchers did not want to confound reading skill with vocabulary knowledge by testing learners who could not read well yet. In their study, Biemiller and Slonim (2001) created a Grade 2 level of words by using words that over 80% of the Grade 4 learners knew.

Dale and O'Rourke relied largely on intuition in deciding what to count in a word family and what meanings to test when more than one meaning of a word was tested. For many high frequency words several different meanings of the words were tested. Some of these were homonyms or homographs, and others were different senses of the word. For the word *point,* ten different uses of the word were tested. It seems that the level of word family was probably close to the flemma. In the following quote *inflections* means forms containing affixes.

> The standard for testing inflections was this: If the inflection is likely to provide a variant score, we should test it. We usually did not test regularly inflected words – the addition of *s, ed, ing, ly*, etc. But we considered retesting if the visual pattern of the word was irregularly changed in the inflecting, for example, *substance* and *substantive*. Lengthening the word did tend to make it "harder" and in the lower grades inflection may make the word less familiar since the affixes might not be known.
> (Dale & O'Rourke, 1981)

If we run the *Living Word Vocabulary* through the BNC/COCA lists (available at <https://www.wgtn.ac.nz/lals/resources/vocabulary-lists>) which use a more inclusive definition of word family and does not distinguish different senses of words, the *Living Word Vocabulary* contains around 18,000 words if proper names, transparent compounds and acronyms are not included. This is certainly a large enough vocabulary to test school children. Biemiller and Slonim analysed the *Living Word Vocabulary* and concluded it contained 17,570 root words, a figure which is very close to 18,000. Biemiller and Slonim note "One of the advantages of sampling vocabulary from the LWV is that it is possible to estimate the number of words known in a relatively clearly defined and educationally relevant population of words" (p. 499).

Biemiller and Slonim's testing procedure involving recall of a meaning required stronger knowledge of a word than the meaning-recognition multiple-choice tests used by Dale and O'Rourke. However, Biemiller says that they were very liberal in what they accepted as a correct answer.

The Picture Vocabulary Size Test

The Picture Vocabulary Size Test is a test of receptive listening vocabulary size. The test measures whether the test-taker can choose a suitable meaning (a picture) for a given partly contextualised word form presented in a short non-defining context. It is a meaning-recognition test primarily intended for young pre-literate native-speakers up to eight years old and young non-native-speakers of English. There are two versions of the test using different items but following the same design procedures. The test was designed by Paul Nation and programmed by Laurence Anthony. Mark Toomer kindly recorded all the spoken sentences for the tests. Jannie van Hees played an important role in trialling the test. The pictures come from Shutterstock. The following description of the test is largely taken from the more detailed specifications for the test which come with the test.

The Picture Vocabulary Size Test works on an ordinary computer, a touch screen computer, or a tablet. A mouse can be used as well as touching the screen. There are two versions of the test each containing 96 test items. Figure 4.1 shows an example from the test testing the word *beneath*.

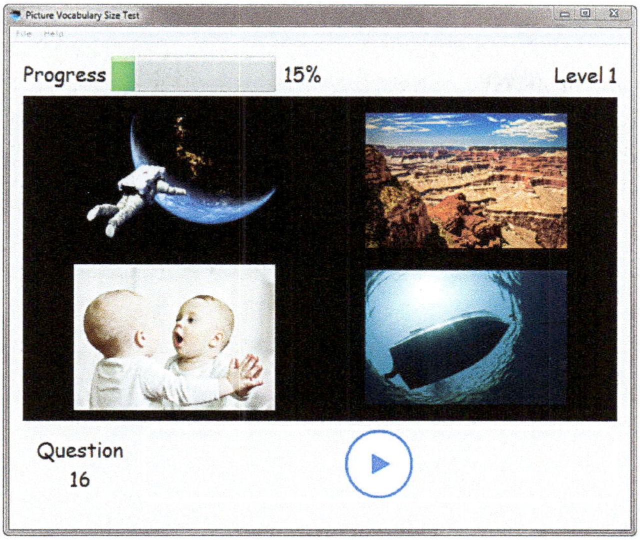

Figure 4.1 An example of the Picture Vocabulary Size Test testing *beneath*

For young native-speakers of English and young learners of English as a foreign or second language, the test can be used as a measure of vocabulary size. The test is based on the most frequent 6000 word-families of English for young native-speaking children. There is likely to be a ceiling effect on the test scores if the test is used with native-speakers of English who are more than seven or eight years old. This is because older learners will be likely to have a substantially larger vocabulary size than that shown by the test.

There is no time limit on the test. It takes around 15 minutes to sit the whole test, but experience shows that some learners may take as long as 25 minutes, agonizing over items and giving it their best shot. Native-speaking learners should sit the whole test because even five-year-olds may know words from the 5th and 6th 1000 levels.

The written form of the word and test sentence also appear at the bottom of the screen and literate learners tend to make use of this.

The test is freely downloadable at <http://www.laurenceanthony.net/software/pvst/>.

The test has been trialled with learners as young as five years old and they experienced no difficulties with the format. The test is administered one-on-one with the test administrator sitting next to the child, explaining how to do the test and keeping the child motivated and on task. Unprompted feedback from teachers indicated that the learners enjoyed doing the test.

There is a growing body of research showing that learners differ in the effort they put into doing a test, particularly a low-stakes test (Barry, Horst, Finney, Brown, & Kopp, 2010; Wise & DeMars, 2005, 2010). A lack of effort or engagement results in lower and misleading scores. The use of one-on-one administration with the PVST (see also Coxhead, Nation, Woods & Sim, 2018) is an attempt to counter this.

Making the test

A five million token corpus was created of American and British adult spoken language (three million tokens), films and TV programs (one million tokens), and reading texts for young children (one million tokens). Twelve 500-word-family lists (a total of 6,000 different words) were made using the range and frequency figures from this corpus. The lists were checked and adjusted by comparison with other existing lists, namely the BNC/COCA lists <https://www.wgtn.ac.nz/lals/resources>, the *General Service List* (West, 1955), Biemiller's (2010) *Words Worth Teaching*, and a list from the Oxford Corpus of Children's Writing (Banerji et al., 2012).

There is a crucial difference between the Picture Vocabulary Size Test and other vocabulary tests used with children, such as the Peabody Picture Vocabulary Test (PPVT). Because the Picture Vocabulary Size Test uses a representative sample of words from a given list, it is possible to estimate a child's total vocabulary size from their score on the test. This is not possible with other tests that are not based on a representative sample from a particular list. Such tests can be used to compare learners or groups of learners, and to compare learners with established norms from the test, but they cannot provide an estimate of the total number of words a learner knows. The Picture Vocabulary Size Test can do this. The major limitation is that the lists used for the test stop at the 6000 word-family level. However, learners who know well over 6000 words are likely to be literate, and a different test, the Vocabulary Size Test (Nation & Beglar, 2007; Elgort & Coxhead, 2016; Coxhead, Nation, & Sim, 2014), can be used with such learners. Nonetheless, because of this limitation on the words tested, it is highly likely that any learner's score on the Picture Vocabulary Size Test is an underestimate, at least to a small degree, because for various reasons learners are likely to know some words that do not appear in the twelve 500 word lists developed for this study.

The simple sentences used with each word were made of words from the first 500 word list. Here are some examples.

Behind:	He's behind the car.
By:	He's by the car.
Thirteen:	Thirteen cars.
House:	This is my house.
Wild:	It's wild.
Table:	It's a table.
Grass:	It's grass.

Informal observations of learners sitting the test

The test is administered to one learner at a time with the test administrator sitting next to the learner and interacting with the learner. This is done (1) to make sure the learner knows what to do, (2) to keep the learner on task, and (3) to keep the learner motivated to keep going and do the test well. Let us look at each of these three points in turn.

When administering the test, it is worth having a short checklist to make sure that each learner knows what to do. As well as knowing to touch a picture, each learner needs to know (1) how to listen to a sentence again by touching the number again, and (2) how to change an answer by touching a different picture or touching the number again. What was striking when administering the test was how some of the eight-year-olds were quickly very strategic in their answering, carefully re-listening to sentences. All were happy to do all the test, and a few spontaneously spoke aloud about their thinking processes as they did it.

A few of the six-year olds wanted to rush through the test somewhat in the manner of a video game, but the test administrator restrained them, encouraging them to consider all pictures and to think carefully about their choices.

Using a touch screen computer raises hygiene issues. Some learners put their finger in their mouth, touched the screen, and then put their finger back in their mouth. One put his finger up his nose in a thoughtful way and then touched the screen.

A few of the younger learners thought that when the picture they touched was ringed by the same colour as the box that appeared around the number, this showed they were correct, with one particularly enthusiastic learner punching the air and saying "Yes!" each time.

The "I don't know" option

The question mark indicating "I don't know" was added late in the development of the test. Not all learners wanted to use the "I don't know" option with just under half not using it at all. This variability in the use of "I don't know" has been found in other studies (Zhang, 2013) and indicates it is best not to use this option.

Some data from using the tests

The tests have been used in three New Zealand schools to test six-year-old and eight-year-old learners who were born in New Zealand or in a few cases who had come to New Zealand at a very young age. In New Zealand, schools are classified into deciles (ten levels) according to the incomes of families in the local area, with decile one being the lowest and decile ten being the highest. This is so that schools in lower socio-economic areas can get more government funding. One school in the study was a decile one school with the vast majority of the learners with parents from Samoa, Tonga, Niue and other Pacific islands. The other two schools were decile ten schools with few Polynesian children.

The test was trialled with a few five-year-olds to see if they could manage the test, and a twelve and a thirteen-year-old to make sure that all items could be correctly answered by children who were likely to know them. Most of the five-year-olds coped well with the test, although some were so distracted by particularly attractive pictures that they wanted to touch them even though they knew they were not the right answer. The twelve and thirteen-year-olds made a very small number of errors on *disillusioned* and *obnoxious*.

Six and eight-year-olds were chosen for the age comparison study so that there would be a clear age gap between the two groups of a minimum of twelve months and a maximum of 24 months. Six-year-olds and seven-year-olds for example can differ in age by only a few days if their birthdays are close to each other, as can seven and eight-year-olds. Similarly, the extremes of decile one and decile ten schools were chosen to get a clear contrast.

Table 4.2 presents the results of using the tests in three different schools.

Table 4.2 Vocabulary size scores from three schools at two decile levels and two age levels

Decile & school	6 year olds mean vocab size (s.d.)	8 year olds mean vocab size (s.d.)
1 School 1	3539 (649)	4540 (488)
10 School 2	4044 (593)	5056 (388)
10 School 3	3924 (398)	4990 (351)

The average age increase is around 500 words per year. Decile 10 children are on average 500 words (one year) ahead of decile 1 children. The standard deviations decrease with age, but this may also be the result of a ceiling effect. Similarly, the yearly increase of 500 words rather than 1000 words is also likely to be the result of a ceiling effect.

The Picture Vocabulary Size Test draws on a much smaller population of words than Biemiller and Slonim's tests. The single advantage of the Picture Vocabulary

Size Test over Biemiller and Slonim's test is that the multiple-choice picture format provides a more reliable way of testing and gives young children the greatest chance of showing what they know. However, the Picture Vocabulary Size Test has limited use as a test of total vocabulary size.

The testing that has been done on the receptive vocabulary size of young school children fits with the counts of the productive vocabulary size of very young pre-school children that we looked at in Chapter 2. Young native-speakers of English begin school knowing several thousand words and increase their vocabulary size each year by close to 1000 words. Furthermore, the vocabulary growth and sizes of primary school children also fits with the vocabulary growth and vocabulary sizes of teen-agers at secondary school, following the rough rule of thumb of a vocabulary size increase of around 1000 word families per year from three-years-old on, with variation of around two thousand words each side of this average.

CHAPTER 5

The vocabulary sizes of native-speakers of English in secondary school

Research by Thorndike (1924); Biemiller (2005) and Biemiller and Slonim (2001), and Dale and O'Rourke's (1981) ratings of vocabulary knowledge suggest that, by the end of primary school around the age of twelve or thirteen, young native-speakers of English have a vocabulary size of around 10,000–11,000 word families.

In this chapter we look at the vocabulary sizes of teen-agers at secondary school using a test based on word frequency lists – the Vocabulary Size Test developed by Paul Nation. This test is based on frequency lists of word families developed initially from data from the British National Corpus (BNC), and later enriched with data from the Corpus of Contemporary American English (COCA).

An important theme in this chapter is that for a reasonable number of learners there is great value in administering the test individually, with the test administrator sitting next to the test-taker and keeping them motivated and on task, so that the results of the test represent the best that they can do.

The Vocabulary Size Test

The Vocabulary Size Test measures vocabulary size up to the 20th 1000 word families. There are six test versions. Some versions are available from Paul Nation's web page. Each of the twenty 1000 word levels in the test is represented by 5 items, and so each test contains 100 items. Here is a sample item.

5. compost: We need some **compost**.
   a. strong support
   b. help to feel better
   c. hard stuff made of stones and sand stuck together
   d. rotted plant material

Note that a reasonably precise knowledge of the meaning of the word is required in order to get the correct answer, because all the choices are the same part of speech, they can all fit into the non-defining context given in the test, and some incorrect choices (see choice c) have a slight meaning relationship to the correct answer.

There is a detailed set of specifications that accompanies the test (see Paul Nation's web page) and analyses of the test can be found in Elgort and Coxhead (2016); Nation & Beglar (2007); Beglar (2010), and Coxhead, Nation, & Sim (2014). The limitations of the test as a measure to be used with non-native-speakers of English are explored in Stoeckel, McLean, & Nation (2020). A web-based version of the test can be found at <www.my.vocabularysize.com>.

The BNC/COCA lists

The test is based on the BNC/COCA word lists which have been in continual development since the early 1990s. There is an analysis of the lists in Nation (2016 Chapter 13) and research on the lists in Dang & Webb (2016) and Dang, Webb, & Coxhead (2020). There is a description of the lists called *Information on the BNC_COCA word family lists* available from Paul Nation's web page.

The lists are largely range and frequency based using frequency and range data from the British National Corpus (BNC) and the Corpus of Contemporary American English (COCA). However, particularly for the first 3000 words, there has been a lot of adjustment based on lexical sets such as survival vocabulary (Nation & Crabbe, 1991), numbers, days of the week, months of the year, seasons and points of the compass, and based on checking with a very large number of other corpora and lists including those involving spoken language.

The unit of counting is Level 6 of Bauer and Nation (1993). Level 6 involves stems which are free forms and 91 affixes. This means that *accuse, accuser, accusation, accusingly* are members of the same family because they all share the same free-standing stem *accuse*. On the other hand, *aberrance, aberration,* and *aberrant* are members of different families because they do not share a free-standing stem (*aber* and *aberr* are not English words). The main justification for counting words in word families is that knowledge of one member of the family makes it easier to deal with other members of the family when met in reading or listening. When testing, the stem form of the family is usually chosen except if one of the family members which is a derived form is much more frequent, for example *computer* would be chosen instead of the stem *compute*.

As we shall see in Chapter 6, Brysbaert, Stevens, Mandera, and Keuleers (2016) considered that for native-speakers of English, word families should also be made with stems which are bound forms which would put all of the forms beginning with *aberr* given above in the same family.

The BNC/COCA lists include separate lists of proper names, marginal words (exclamations, affixes, swear words, letters of the alphabet), transparent compounds, acronyms, and foreign words. The justifications for these various lists and the criteria for inclusion in them are described in Nation (2016). When sampling for the Vocabulary Size Tests, these separate lists were not sampled from. The goal in developing the BNC/COCA lists has been to have lists of words up to the 30th 1000 without including large numbers of highly technical words. It is a difficult goal to reach and at the time of writing this book, the lists go up to the 28th 1000.

The lists have been used for corpus-based research looking at the proportions of different levels of vocabulary in various kinds of texts, for setting vocabulary learning goals for non-native-learners of English (see for example Nation, 2016), and for sampling for vocabulary size testing (see for example Webb, Sasao, & Ballance, 2017).

Using the Vocabulary Size Test in New Zealand secondary schools

Coxhead, Nation, and Sim (2015) and Coxhead, Nation, Woods, and Sim (2018) used the 100 item Vocabulary Size Test (Versions C and E) based on the first 20,000 BNC/COCA word families to measure the vocabulary size of New Zealand secondary school students, who ranged in age from 13 to 17 years old. As well as measuring vocabulary size, the study also had the aim of comparing the effects of individual testing and group testing. In individual one-on-one testing, a test administrator sat next to the test-taker giving encouragement and keeping them on task. In group testing, several test-takers took the test with just one test administrator overseeing the test and giving help where requested.

The results in Table 5.1 are for the individually administered tests. Because the tests involved a 1 in 200 sample from the lists of 20,000 word-families, each learner's raw score on the test of 100 items was multiplied by 200 to estimate their vocabulary size.

Table 5.1 The vocabulary sizes of secondary school students

Age	Average vocabulary size (s.d.)	Lowest and highest sizes
13	10,800 (2,253)	6,600–15,200
14	11,500 (2,341)	6,400–15,600
15	11,800 (2,029)	7000–16,200
16	13,100 (1,653)	9,400–15,600
17	13,400 (1,548)	10,000–17,000

The lowest and highest scores show the extremes. Most learners were within 2,000 words each side of the average.

The points to note are, firstly, the results are based on the individually administered tests, so each learner had a good chance to demonstrate what they knew. Secondly, even the lowest scoring learner knew at least 6,400 words. Native-speakers of English know thousands of words. Thirdly, learners of the same age can differ greatly in their vocabulary size. While vocabulary size increases with age, age is probably a surrogate for breadth of experience, and learners who read more than others of their same age, who engage in a wider range of activities and whose families have enough income to do lots of different things are likely to have larger vocabulary sizes. Fourthly, the rough rule of thumb (age minus 2, times 1000; see Chapter 1) does not fit so well with this data. The rule of thumb is closer to age minus 3, times 1000.

We will look again at factors affecting the growth of vocabulary size and affecting the measurement of vocabulary size in Chapter 7. However, the study did not show gender differences for vocabulary size.

The role of test-taking effort

Learners whose vocabulary sizes were at the lower ranges for their age performed substantially better on an individually-administered test than on a group-administered test.

For obvious time and resource-saving reasons, most tests are typically administered to a large group of learners (a whole class) at the same time with one administrator. Unfortunately, the scores on a group-administered test may depend not only on what the learners know, but also on how much effort they put into sitting the test. Informal work reported in Nation (2007b) with the Vocabulary Levels Test (Nation, 2013; Schmitt, Schmitt, & Clapham, 2001) in New Zealand schools made it clear that many learners did not try their best when sitting low stakes tests. When the whole class sat a test administered by the teacher, some of the learners did not try their hardest and their attention was not strongly focused on the test. As a result, their test scores did not fully reflect their knowledge. The learners tended to rush through the test, not using sensible test-taking strategies, and generally not giving it their best shot. The learners who were most likely to do this were those who tended to be struggling at school, and their poor results on the poorly taken test reinforced both their and their teachers' impressions of their inadequacy.

When a test administrator sat with an individual learner as the learner sat the test keeping them on task, their scores were much higher (Nation, 2007b). It was thus clear that for some learners the results of a group-administered test were misleading and strongly demotivating. Because we wanted to get the clearest picture of learners' vocabulary size, we needed to make sure that the test gave learners the best chance of showing what they really knew. Although individual test administration is extremely time-consuming, there was no point in giving group-administered tests if the results were meaningless for many of the test takers.

Thus, a very important aim of the research was to compare the effects of group administered and individually-administered tests.

It is self-evident that the more attention learners give to a task, the better they will do it. While there is no research on this in vocabulary testing, there is evidence supporting it in assessment in a variety of disciplines. Wise and DeMars (2005) in a review of studies define *test-taking effort* as "a student's engagement and expenditure of energy toward the goal of attaining the highest possible score on the test" (p. 2). The term *test-taking motivation* is used in some studies. Particularly on low-stakes tests, a student's score depends not only on the knowledge they bring to the test, but also on their test-taking effort (Barry, Horst, Finney, Brown, & Kopp, 2010; Segal, 2012; Wise & DeMars, 2005, 2010). This effort can be largely explained by an expectancy-value model where the motivation with which a student approaches a task depends on their expectancy of being able to complete the task successfully, and the value that they see in completing the task (Wigfield & Eccles, 2000). If students see the task as being one that they are capable of doing, and if they see some intrinsic or extrinsic value in doing the task well, they are likely to do the task well. If, however, they see the task as being too difficult and/or not being of any interest or value to them, they are likely to skip through the task as quickly as possible not giving it their full attention. Low motivation leads to low test scores. Wise and DeMars (2005) point out that test-taking effort affects test validity. If students do not truly show what they know, then the test is not fully measuring what it is supposed to measure.

Researchers have investigated test-taking effort in a variety of ways. It has been measured using questionnaires (Barry et al., 2010; Liu, Bridgeman & Adler, 2012), and item response times on a computerised test (Wise & DeMars, 2010). Segal (2012) measured test-taking effort experimentally by getting students to do a matching task that did not involve previous learning but depended on how well they devoted themselves to the task.

A variety of methods have been used to increase test-taking effort, such as providing monetary rewards (O'Neil, Abedi, Miyoshi, & Mastergeorge, 2005), making assessment count in awarding grades or reporting results (increasing the stakes) (Liu, Rios, & Borden, 2015), making tests easier, making tests interesting and challenging, and providing feedback. Another possibility is to individually monitor learners as they sit the test so that their performance is continually observed and commented on. This is the approach used in the present study.

In our study, we made efforts to maximise test-taking effort by making sure the test takers were focused on the test, paying attention, taking it seriously, keeping on task by getting help with problems that arose during the test and encouraged to keep working. Test takers working without this support may also remain engaged and on task, but there is a greater likelihood that this will happen if test takers are individually supported.

Coxhead, Nation, Woods and Sim (2018) used two versions of the Vocabulary Size Test (versions C and E) which had been shown in a previous study to have statistically comparable means (Coxhead, Nation & Sim, 2014). Each learner sat both versions of the test, one individually administered and one administered in a group.

Group and individual testing conditions and test order were assigned randomly. In the individual administration, an administrator sat next to the test-taker as she or he answered the test questions on a computer or on paper. The administrator gave encouragement and praise, pronounced words when asked, and generally kept the learner on task. In the group administration, the test-takers answered the test questions on computer or on paper in groups of between six and thirty people in classrooms. The administrator handed out the tests or set up the tests on laptops or computers, monitored the participants, answered any questions about the test including pronunciation of words if requested (except for the meaning of the test items), and collected the scripts. Instructions for the administrators are in Appendix 1.

There was an order effect on the tests with learners generally scoring higher on the second test.

The aim of the study was to see if the effects of the two ways of administering the test were different for those students who had relatively low scores on the group-administered Vocabulary Size Test for their age compared with those who had relatively high scores. To make this comparison, the students at each of five ages (13–17-years-old) were divided into quartiles based on their scores on the group-administered test. Since these tests are most often conducted in a group setting, and since "normal" ranges are most often quoted by age, we split the students into quartiles based on their group scores and their age. That is, students aged 13 who were in the lowest 25% of their age group were designated as quartile one, as were 14-year-old students who were in the lowest 25% of their age group, and so on for ages up to 17. Students aged 13 who were in the second 25% were placed in the second quartile as were students aged 14 who were in the second 25% of their age group and so on. So, in each quartile there were students from all age levels.

The individual test score is significantly higher for quartiles one and two, and there is a small-to-medium sized effect observed in the third group. For quartile one (those with the lowest group test scores for their age group) there was a difference of 8.6 points which is a difference in vocabulary size of 1700 word families. This is a big difference. For the second quartile, the individual results were on average 2.78 points higher than the group scores. For the third quartile, the individual results were on average 1.84 points higher than the group scores, and this represents a small-to-medium sized effect ($p = .051$). For the highest quartile, the individual results were on average 0.23 points higher than the group scores but this difference was not statistically significant. The fourth quartile students did not benefit from having individual testing and it may have even had a small negative effect on scores of some of these students.

Table 5.2 The difference between supported and unsupported testing for students at four different vocabulary proficiency levels

Quartile	Individual mean	Group mean	Difference
1	49.29	40.93	8.36
2	54.48	51.70	2.78
3	62.97	61.13	1.84
4	71.77	71.54	0.23

Clearly the effect of individual administration is strong enough to make a big difference for the lowest 25% of the students, and this effect persists at least to a small degree for another 50% of the students. Converting points to word families means that 8.36 points is equivalent to 1,672 word families (8.36 times 200), 2.78 points to 556 word families, and 1.84 points to 368 word families. If we relate this difference to the group scores (40.93), then learners in the first quartile sitting the individually administered test (49.29) increased their scores by well over 8%. Fourteen learners (12.6%) had much higher scores in individual administration (10 points out of 100 or higher). If group-administered Vocabulary Size Tests are used, at least one-quarter of the students in schools like the ones in this study are likely to have misleading results greatly under-estimating their vocabulary size. The schools in this study were in moderate to high socio-economic areas. These results are likely to be even more misleading in schools in lower socio-economic areas, because vocabulary knowledge is closely related to socio-economic status (Farkas & Beron, 2004).

It is not easy to isolate the various effects of one-on-one individual administration. However, experience in administering such tests suggests that the following ranked list of factors accounts for most effects. The most influential factor is given first. The first two factors cover test-taking effort.

1. The learners give their full attention to the task. This means that they do their best to answer the questions and are not distracted by other factors. This is a direct result of having the full attention of the test administrator.
2. The learners are encouraged to remain positive about their chances of answering items correctly. This is encouraged by positive comments from the test administrator.

3. The learners are able to clarify aspects of the task such as whether they should answer items they are unsure about and clarify aspects of individual items such as the pronunciation of some of the words. The test administrator can provide needed information excluding, of course, the meaning of the word.
4. The learners are encouraged to take a strategic approach to answering the test items applying what test-wiseness skills they have.

Individually administered tests are largely impractical for more than a few learners. Teachers who are concerned about their low scoring students could possibly use a group administration first for screening purposes and then an individual administration to see more accurately what these students know and can do.

The secondary school test results show that learners continue to increase their vocabulary size during their teen-age years. Because secondary school students have larger vocabulary sizes than primary school students, the individual differences in vocabulary size between secondary school students is also larger. The rough rule of thumb still applies to the majority of the students, but there are striking differences at the extremes between those who, for example, struggle with school and with reading and those who are reading way beyond their age level and who excel at school. Nonetheless, even the students with the lowest vocabulary sizes know several thousand words, and their vocabulary size will continue to grow. In Chapter 8 we will look at ways in which this growth can be supported and encouraged.

CHAPTER 6

Frequency-list based studies of adult native-speakers' vocabulary size

The Vocabulary Size Test is a frequency-list based test. One of the strengths of tests based on frequency lists is that the validity of the lists can now be checked by running them over several very large corpora to make sure that the lists contain all the words that native-speakers are likely to know. In spite of this, vocabulary size tests for adults are likely to underestimate their vocabulary size in some cases because such tests typically do not test specialised vocabularies such as the very large vocabularies of medicine or botany, or the smaller but equally specialised vocabularies of computer programming or building. Medicine seems to have a technical vocabulary approaching 10,000 words (Quero, 2015). Smaller technical vocabularies are likely to be around 1000–2000 words depending on how *technical* is defined, and whether multiword units are included in the technical vocabulary.

The studies examined in this chapter focus on non-technical vocabulary using frequency-based word lists. The tests mainly focused on adults although not exclusively so.

Test your own wordpower

In 1975 Hunter Diack in conjunction with J. C. Daniels published a book called *Standard Literacy Tests* (Diack, 1975a). This was very soon after repackaged as *Test your own Wordpower* intended for a wider market. This book consists of a long introduction and fifty tests, each testing 60 words divided into six levels of 10 words. Here is the first of the fifty tests.

Level 1	Level 2	Level 3
1 abroad	11 abandon	21 abridge
2 binoculars	12 ballot	22 aggregate
3 daily	13 chaos	23 bivouac
4 expedition	14 contraband	24 chronology
5 horizon	15 excavate	25 credulous
6 jungle	16 fatigue	26 hireling
7 limit	17 laboratory	27 indolent
8 pattern	18 manual	28 meagre
9 rate	19 purchase	29 nomadic
10 stroke	20 shuttle	30 occidental
Level 4	**Level 5**	**Level 6**
31 abhorrent	41 abscissa	51 aboulia
32 amorphous	42 badinage	52 bicuspid
33 crustacean	43 cartel	53 caracole
34 declivity	44 daemon	54 chalybeate
35 emaciated	45 dendrite	55 croton
36 fabrication	46 exordium	56 dysphoria
37 galaxy	47 inchoate	57 gazebo
38 heretical	48 moraine	58 kymograph
39 igneous	49 rubric	59 ortolan
40 nomenclature	50 soutane	60 quadrat

Figure 6.1 Test 1 from Diack's (1975b) *Test your own Wordpower*

Each word in the tests represents 600 words so a person's score on a test should be multiplied by 600 to estimate their total vocabulary size. The highest possible estimate if every word in a test was known would be 36,000. Diack recommended taking the average of at least three tests to get a reliable estimate.

Diack suggested a procedure for taking each test. "Read through the tests in the order as numbered. When you come to a word to which you cannot give at least one acceptable meaning, enter the number of that word in one of the ten squares printed below. Then carry on reading through the test until you come to the next word you are not sure of. Enter the number of that word in the next square. Carry on in the same way until you have filled all the squares with a number. At that point stop reading through the test." The test-taker then had to write a meaning of some form for each of the five last words they considered they knew. They then checked the meanings in a dictionary and if all were correct, then their score on the test was all the words they said they knew. Diack's tests were basically Yes/No tests with a self-checking procedure on the lowest frequency items said to be known. *Yes* means "I could give a meaning for this word."

Diack considered on the basis of his experience with the tests that intellectually curious 20-year-olds would have a vocabulary size around 18,000 to 24,000 word families and in some cases even higher. Diack also suggested that a person's vocabulary grew at a rate of several hundred words or even a thousand word families a year for as long as formal education goes on. Table 6.1 gives Diack's interpretation of scores on his tests.

Table 6.1 Diack's six levels and the types of people at each level

Vocabulary level and sizes	People gaining such scores
Level 1: 0–6,000 words	Children between the ages of 6 to 9 and illiterate adults
Level 2: 6,000–12,000 words	Bright 10 year olds; around one-quarter of the adult population
Level 3: 12,000–18,000 words	Adults who left school as early as possible; 18 year-olds intending to go on to further education
Level 4: 18,000–24,000 words	Mature adults who read widely; university graduates; members of most professions with some experience
Level 5: 24,000–30,000 words	People who read a lot; people who are at the top of their professions or heading that way
Level 6: 30,000–36,000 words	Similar to Level 5 but only more so.

Diack knew of Thorndike's 30,000 word list but was rather scornful of the usefulness of frequency as a criterion for ranking words, partly because the small corpus size used did not do much to rank the lower frequency words. He was also aware of the dangers of sampling from a dictionary. According to Diack, his moment of insight was when he realised that words were typically learned in a particular order. He then started classifying vocabulary into six levels. He intended at first to have ten levels but found that six levels worked better than ten. Although words at Level 1 (the most well-known 6000 word families) may differ from individual to individual, the differences are probably constrained within a range of 12,000 words. Diack's criterion of order of learning is very similar to Keuleers, Stevens, Mandera, & Brysbaert's (2015) criterion of "prevalence" – the percentage of a population knowing a word.

Diack used dictionaries to create his six levels, along with Roget's thesaurus and Thorndike and Lorge's (1944) word list. He stresses that his tests were tests of general vocabulary and do not give credit for knowledge of highly technical terms or dialect words (p. 27), although he acknowledges the difficulty of separating general and technical terms. He generally let the dictionaries decide if a word was highly technical through its non-occurrence in the dictionaries. One of the reasons that Diack's study is included in this chapter is because as well as his intuition he used the Thorndike and Lorge frequency based list as guide when classifying words into his six levels. He also mainly focused on adults.

Diack does not give his criteria for deciding what is in a word family, but his families clearly include some derived forms as family members, and homographs and homonyms were not counted as different words. His tests do not include proper names or acronyms. It seems that his target of 36,000 words was to some degree determined by the *Concise Oxford Dictionary* as he initially calculated that that contained that number of words. The exclusion of homographs and homonyms reduced that figure considerably, but their loss was compensated for by including non-transparent compound words which are not headwords in the *Concise Oxford Dictionary*. "Throughout the dictionary there were enough of these, I felt, to justify my estimate of 36,000 words as the measuring-rod for general vocabulary." (p. 21). When looking through his tests however, there seem to be few compound words, barely one per test, and it may be that Diack's 36,000 word estimate of a population of words to sample from to measure vocabulary size may have been a little too large, and if he had used a smaller estimate, his figures would have been more in line with the later Goulden, Nation, and Read (1990) study. This suggests that Diack did not make a list of 36,000 words to sample from, but he created his tests using his six intuitive levels of order of learning. He presumably assigned 3,000 words to these levels in order to make his 50 tests with 60 words per test. His tests also contain a reasonable number of derived forms as test words. In Figure 6.1 we can see the derived forms *hireling, nomadic, occidental, abhorrent, fabrication, heretical* and the inflected form *emaciated*. These would all be family members at Level 6 in Bauer and Nation (1993) and thus not counted as separate words.

Although Diack's words came from dictionaries, he avoided sampling problems by using his six levels. However, we do not know if indeed there were 6,000 words at each level. It also seems that the words chosen for the tests, particularly in Levels 1 to 3, did not represent a range of degrees of familiarity within a level, but represented the words that could occur at the upper boundary of each level. When commenting on the word *rat* and its various uses, he notes that this word "is normally learned so early in life that it does not qualify for inclusion even at Level 1" (p. 20).

In spite of the mildly eccentric, intuitive nature of their construction, Diack's tests provide reliable, reasonably accurate estimates of vocabulary size. They represent a remarkable very practical achievement that avoided most of the errors of the previous research on native-speaker vocabulary size.

Using several forms of the same test

Part of the long development of the Vocabulary Size Test involved the creation of parallel forms of the test. Coxhead, Nation, and Sim (2014) looked at the performance of six forms of the test, many created by Brian King under a research grant won by Averil Coxhead, using data on vocabulary size gathered largely from university students of various ages. Having parallel forms of a test provides a way of checking the reliability of the test. It also allows re-testing of the same learners under different conditions to see the effects of those conditions on test results. It also allows some tests to be made available for teachers and learners to use, and allows some to be kept unfamiliar and inaccessible so that they can be used for future research.

Ideally, equivalent forms of a test should all be made at the same time following the same criteria. Inevitably, equivalent forms are never truly equivalent, but they can get fairly close. Equivalent forms of a test are based on equivalence between groups. Although they can have very similar means and standard deviations for groups, an individual's score on two equivalent tests can differ by several points. Coxhead, Nation, and Sim (2014) checked this for six versions of the Vocabulary Size Test and found that 80% of the learners had scores that were less than 5 points apart. As each point represented 200 word families, a five point or higher difference would mean a 1000 word family difference in estimating vocabulary size. In studies using two or more measures of vocabulary size at different times, where individual scores matter, it may be safer to use the same test twice and risk a carry-over effect rather than to use two different versions. In group comparisons, however, using different equivalent versions of the test would be fine.

The criteria followed when making the tests included first using random numbers to select items from each of the first 20 BNC word family lists created by Paul Nation. Then a short non-defining context was created for each word using largely words in the first 500 words of English. The third step was to choose the three distractors for each item. These distractors should be from the same 1000 word-family list as the tested word. At this point the placement of the correct answer was decided, so that there would be a rough balance of A, B, C, and D correct answers across the whole test. When choosing the distractors, care was taken to make sure that the distractors were not too distracting. That is, the distractors should share the same part of speech as the tested word, but they should not share important elements of meaning. When choosing or writing the distractors, it may be necessary to alter the non-defining context sentence for the tested word, usually in a small way, if it is too restrictive. The choices (correct answer and distractors) were all written within the first 3000 words of the lists. On a few occasions, a word from the fourth or fifth 1000 needed to be used, but the words in the choices were always from a higher frequency level than the tested word. The choices were checked to make sure that the length of the choice did not signal the correct answer, and that words like *a/an* were not signalling a choice.

Forty-six university students sat all six versions of the Vocabulary Size Test in one-on-one testing conditions (one supervisor-one test-taker). Twenty-eight were native-speakers of English and eighteen were high-proficiency non-native-speakers. The scores on the tests were checked to see if the means and variances were significantly different from each other. In addition, they were checked to see how much an individual's score would differ if they sat two different versions.

The tests clustered into two groups of three. The data supports the two groupings of parallel versions but shows very clearly that even parallel versions are unlikely to provide identical scores, and for a significant group of test-takers (around 20–30% of the test-takers), the scores on two tests taken by the same person are likely to be several points apart.

The native-speakers averaged around 90 out of 100 (18,000 words) on one cluster of three tests and 86 out of 100 (17,200 words) on the other cluster of three tests. The non-native-speakers with European first languages cognate with English scored much higher than speakers with Asian first languages. Generally, older test-takers had higher scores than younger test-takers. The high scores and the low standard errors on the tests for native-speakers suggest that for university students and graduates, the tests up to the 20th 1000 level have a ceiling effect and it would be worth creating extended versions of the tests up to the 28th 1000 level or higher if the word lists are available.

A massive online measure of English vocabulary knowledge

Brysbaert, Stevens, Mandera, and Keuleers (2016) built a list of English words by using their SUBTLEX word frequency list (made from the subtitles to movies (Brysbaert & New, 2009)) and freely available spellchecker lists. Specialised technical words were excluded resulting in a list that contained 61,800 lemmas. Brysbaert et al. said: "we are fairly confident it contains the vast majority of reasonably known English words (in American English spelling), but we agree that it would be possible to add about the same number of more specialist words" (p. 16). Their lists did not contain proper names or acronyms. Non-transparent compound words were included in the lists, but the criteria for deciding on non-transparency were not explained.

Brysbaert, Stevens, Mandera, and Keuleers wanted to compare the effects of counting lemmas and counting families. A lemma consists of a word and its inflected forms. The strict definition of a lemma is that all members are the same part of speech. A less strict definition and the one used by Brysbaert et al. includes only inflected forms but can include different parts of speech. So, *tread* as a noun and its plural form and *tread* as a verb and its inflections would all be part of the same lemma, sometimes called a *flemma*. Brysbaert, Stevens, Mandera, and Keuleers decided to make the contrast between lemmas and families as extreme as possible. So, rather than using Bauer and Nation's (1993) Level 6 word families as in the BNC/COCA lists where the stem forms of words also exist as independent words (free forms), they chose Level 7 where word stems can be free forms or bound forms. The stem in a bound form does not exist as an independent word. Level 7 is less clearly defined than the other levels because many judgements need to be made. So, for example, all the words *abbacy, abbatial, abbe, abbess, abbey, abbot, abbotship* were all included in the Level 7 word family *abbey*. At Bauer and Nation Level 6, *abbotship* would be part of the *abbot* family, but all the other words, *abbacy, abbatial, abbe, abbess, abbey* would be five separate word families different from the *abbot* word family. While there are no clearly defined rules for making Level 7 families, all the families used in the study are provided for inspection in lists accompanying the article reporting the research. The 61,800 lemmas became 18,269 word families. The assumption behind word families is that knowing one member of the family makes knowledge of other members of the family more accessible.

Using the lemma as the word counting unit is not suitable for testing native-speakers of English because adult native-speakers have no difficulty in seeing that different lemmas like *slow, slowly, slowness* are clearly related to each other. Using bound forms as headwords of word families is more debateable. For example, words sharing the very common bound stem *spect* (e.g. *respect, inspect, spectacles*) were not included in the same family. However, Brysbaert et al. wanted to use the upper and lower bounds of word family size to measure vocabulary size to get a clear picture of the possible range of size figures at various word family sizes. A very important aspect of the study is that it provides a way of checking whether we should be talking about thousands of words, tens of thousands of words, or hundreds of thousands of words when we talk about a native-speaker's vocabulary size.

Do the Brysbaert et al. lists contain all the words they should contain? By checking Brysbaert et al.'s list against the BNC/COCA lists we can try to answer this question. There are very few words in the BNC/COCA first 20,000 which are not in Brysbaert et al.'s lists. Some accidental omissions are *again, against, ahead, alfalfa, nought, monograph, midden* but these are very few and would not affect the test results.

Brysbaert et al. tested the words using Yes/No tests with 100 randomly selected words in each test – 67 words and 33 pseudo-words. The pseudo-words were used as checks on test-takers' response accuracy. The proportion of yes-responses to the nonwords was subtracted from the proportion of yes-responses to the words. The test-takers knew that their tests would contain pseudo-words. The test-takers were asked to indicate which words they knew. Brysbaert et al. note: "This knowledge can be as shallow as knowing that the word exists." (p. 2). The advantages of Yes/No tests are that they are easy to make, quick and easy to administer and score, and have been well-researched. Their disadvantage is that they can be answered using minimal knowledge of the word.

Crowd-sourcing through the internet was used, so an enormous number of people were tested, 221,268 individuals covering all of the 61,800 words in the lemma list. Data was also collected on the participants' age, level of education and languages known.

Knowledge of word families was calculated by using knowledge of the family headword, or in the case of families involving a bound stem by using knowledge of the full word in the family which had the highest recognition rate.

According to Brysbaert et al., twenty-year-olds know around 11,100 word families (the median) with vocabulary sizes ranging from 6,100 to 14,900 word families. Sixty-year-olds know around 13,400 word families with vocabulary sizes ranging from 9,000 to 16,700 word families. The median results expressed in lemmas were 42,000 lemmas for twenty-year-olds and 48,200 lemmas for sixty year olds. It is worth remembering that Brysbaert et al.'s definition of a word family was much more inclusive than that used for the BNC/COCA word families and so the vocabulary size scores were much lower than those estimated by the rule of thumb. The Brysbaert et al. study drew from a total population of 18,269 words, while the BNC/COCA lists include around 28,000 word families. Most of this difference is a result of the definition of word family.

We saw that the vocabulary sizes of teen-agers can cover a wide range at the same age. Adults' vocabulary sizes at the same age similarly cover a wide range.

Data gathered from online versions of the Vocabulary Size Test

Myq Larson created an online version of the Vocabulary Size Test and his data-gathering included over 47,000 native-speakers of English (Larson, 2019). Figure 6.2 shows this data. Note the similarity between this graph and Figure 7.2 illustrating Heap's Law.

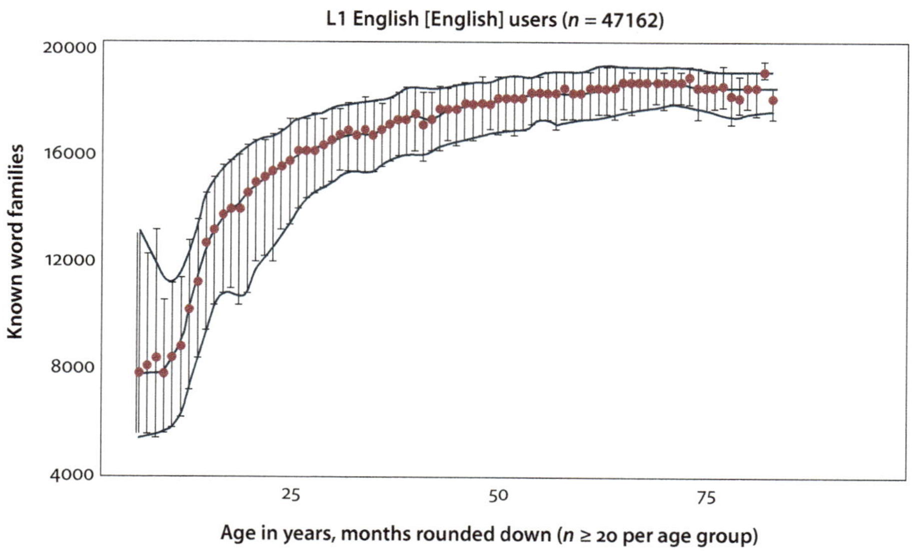

Figure 6.2 Native-speaker scores at various ages on the Vocabulary Size Test

At each age group between the ages of 15 and 26 there were over 1000 test-takers, and over 500 up to the age of 68. Table 6.2 contains data for every 5th year of age. Data for each year can be found at <http://www.vocabularysize.net/iallt2019/iallt.html>.

Table 6.2 Average vocabulary sizes at different age levels from the Vocabulary Size Test at my.vocabularysize.com

Age	Vocab size	s.d.	Increase
10	8,009	3818	
15	12,101	3582	4,092
20	13,199	4245	1,098
25	14,556	3879	1,235
30	15,791	2975	1,225
35	15,961	3254	170
40	16,742	2677	781
45	17,138	2132	396
50	17,550	1835	412
55	17,946	1523	396
60	17,909	1445	−37
65	18,188	1519	279
70	18,206	1648	18
75	18,046	1419	−160
80	17,935	1354	−111

The increase column on the right shows the increase in the number of different words for the five year period. So, in the five years between the ages of 10 to 15, vocabulary size increases by 4,092 different word families or 818 words per year, from 15 to 30 by just over 200 words per year, and this rate stays much the same until after the age of 30 when the annual rate drops to just over 80 words per year until the age of 55. From the age of 55 to 70 there is a small increase and some signs of attrition, with attrition being more noticeable but small from 75 years on.

This data includes native-speakers from a range of educational levels, and it would be interesting to see if those who engaged in tertiary study made the greatest increases in vocabulary size in the 20 to 30-year-old age range.

Some speculations

It is interesting to speculate what the vocabulary size results would have been if Brysbaert et al., (2016) used the same word family size was used as in the Vocabulary Size Test. Brysbaert et al. were working from 18,269 word families. Coxhead, Nation, and Sim (2014) and Larson (2019) were working with tests based on 20,000 word families but the BNC/COCA lists contain around 28,000 word families. Certainly,

Brysbaert et al.'s results would have been closer to the word family results than the lemma results and seem likely to be around Coxhead, Nation, and Sim's (2014) 18,000 word estimate for university students. This comparison is complicated not only by the different definitions of word family but also by the different test item format used. If the test-takers seriously apply meaning-recall in the Yes/No format it can be a more demanding test than multiple-choice. If they just rely on word-form recognition, it is a much less demanding test than multiple-choice.

As we have seen in earlier chapters, there is very little sound research done on the vocabulary size of native-speakers of English. What is particularly interesting about the studies reviewed in this chapter is that there is a kind of consensus about how many words are likely to be worth testing when measuring non-specialist vocabulary size. The number of words depends on how the membership of the word family is decided. Diack (1975b) had the least inclusive word family and considered he was working with a population of 36,000 words. Nation, Coxhead, and Sim (2104) used carefully described word families that were based on free stems, and were working with a population of close to 28,000 word families, although only 20,000 of these were sampled for testing. Brysbaert, Stevens, Mandera, and Keuleers (2016) had the most restrictive definition of a word family, grouping some words sharing bound stems and in some cases grouping words that were clearly related but which a morphologist would be unlikely to group together. They were working with 18,269 word families.

It seems clear that for adult native-speakers of English, we need to use a word family definition somewhere within Bauer and Nation's (1993) Level 7 which allows the use of bound stems in some word families and we need to use tests that draw on a population of words somewhere around the 25,000 word level. This suggests that adult native-speakers of English who have completed substantial tertiary education are likely to have a general vocabulary size of close to 20,000 word families with an additional specialist vocabulary size ranging from a few hundred words to several thousand words depending on the discipline studied. Most additional technical vocabularies will be around 1000 words if multiword units where the words are separated by spaces are not counted. A small number of professionals such as doctors, botanists and chemists may have larger specialist vocabularies of up to 10,000 words. We have at least a rough idea now of the size of the ball-park.

CHAPTER 7

Factors affecting native-speaker vocabulary size and growth

In the previous chapters we have looked at the small amount of research on the vocabulary sizes of native-speakers of English at various age levels that has applied methodologically-sound procedures for measuring vocabulary size. We have found mixed support for what we have called "the rough rule of thumb" that a native-speaker's vocabulary grows at the rate of around 1000 word families a year from about the age of three until about the age of 20 or so. We have also found consistent evidence that the degree of variation around this rough average can be quite large, although most native-speakers eventually know many thousands of word families.

In this chapter, we look at the factors that affect the vocabulary size and growth of native-speakers of a language.

The conditions affecting vocabulary learning

Vocabulary learning occurs as the direct result of the quantity and quality of meetings with unfamiliar and partly known vocabulary. It is necessary to include both unfamiliar and partly known vocabulary in this statement, because learning most words is a cumulative process with various bits of knowledge about each word being strengthened and enriched as the result of various meetings with the word. The quantity of meetings with vocabulary thus refers to the opportunity to meet new vocabulary and the opportunity to meet that vocabulary again several times in order for knowledge of the words to be enriched and established. Learning is affected by repetition, but the quality of initial meetings and more importantly subsequent meetings also has a strong effect on learning. Hoff and Naigles (2002 p. 423) note:

> three different data-providing properties of input are related to children's vocabulary development: sheer frequency of presentation, number of different words, and richness and variety of linguistic environments in which the words are placed.

The quality of meetings with vocabulary can be classified into several levels called learning conditions (Webb & Nation, 2017, Chapter 4). These conditions are listed in Table 7.1 and include noticing, retrieval, varied encounters and varied use, and elaboration. Each of these conditions can occur in incidental learning or in deliberate learning. It is not easy to draw a consistent line between incidental and deliberate learning and for the present we will focus mainly on incidental learning, that is, learning that occurs when the main focus of the learner is on communication rather than vocabulary learning.

Table 7.1 Conditions for vocabulary learning

Quantity of meetings	**Initial occurrence/repetition**	
Quality of attention	**Incidental attention**	**Deliberate attention**
Noticing	Guessing from context	Dictionary look-up
Receptive or productive retrieval	Repeated listening or speaking	Flash card learning
Varied meetings (receptive) or varied use (productive)	Extensive listening or reading	Vocabulary exercises
Receptive or productive elaboration	High-stakes communication	Word part analysis

At the most superficial level, there is the condition of noticing. Noticing may occur when learners meet an unfamiliar word. Noticing also occurs when learners guess the meaning of a word using form, context or background knowledge clues. Noticing occurs when learners negotiate the meaning of a word with each other as a part of spoken communication. Noticing also occurs when learners look up the meaning of a word. Noticing may be a rather superficial condition but it is also a very important condition because it can result in learning that sets up the opportunity for more thoughtful conditions such as retrieval and varied meetings to occur later.

Retrieval occurs when a learner meets a word again and tries to recall the meaning of the word. This kind of retrieval, which occurs in listening and reading, is called receptive retrieval. A more demanding kind of retrieval, productive retrieval, occurs when the learner needs to say or write a word and tries to recall the spoken or written form of the word to express the meaning they want to express. Each successful retrieval strengthens the link between form and meaning and also strengthens knowledge of the form and the meaning. The most effective retrievals for learning are spaced retrievals where the retrievals of the same meaning or form are not done immediately one after the other but are separated.

Retrieval is more effective for learning if the retrievals occur under different circumstances from the previous meetings. These retrievals are called varied encounters and varied use to distinguish receptive and productive retrievals and to emphasize the different circumstances. When learners read or listen, they may hear a partly familiar word again. Typically, the collocations, the sentence context or the referents of the word will be different from previous meetings. The morphological form of the word may be different – singular rather than plural, past tense rather than present, or as an *-ly* adverb rather than as an adjective. These variations on the same word enrich knowledge of the word and make the meeting with the word more memorable (Joe, 1998). When learners speak or write, they may need to use a partly familiar word in circumstances which are different from previous meetings. This varied productive use strengthens and enriches knowledge of the word.

So far, we have looked at the quality conditions of noticing, retrieval, and varied meetings and varied use. These conditions account for a lot of vocabulary learning by native-speakers. However, the deepest quality condition is elaboration. The most obvious examples of elaboration involve deliberate learning rather than incidental learning. These include analysing words to see their word parts, relating different senses of a word to see the core meaning of the word, using a mnemonic technique to help remember a word, and relating a word to a picture or real objects or activities. However, incidental elaboration also occurs when learners are working with language to do things such as make models, cook a cake, give directions or follow an explanation. These activities strongly relate language and actions and can involve instantiation where learners see or visualise particular instances of the meanings of words. There is plenty of evidence that native-speakers subconsciously analyse words into parts, extend the use of words in line with their core meaning, and use rules when pronouncing or writing words.

The two broad conditions of quantity and quality of meetings with words are needed for vocabulary learning to occur. However, these conditions depend on other factors, and in the rest of this chapter we look at these factors as parts of a model of factors affecting vocabulary size and growth, and we relate research on native-speaker vocabulary growth to this model.

A model of factors affecting vocabulary size and growth

There are two major factors that affect the trajectory (or the rough rule of thumb) of vocabulary growth, and these are represented by the upper and lower boxes in the model in Figure 7.1. They are age and the statistical nature of vocabulary. Both age and the statistical nature of vocabulary affect the conditions for vocabulary learning that we have just discussed, and the vertical arrows in Figure 7.1 indicate this.

There is a series of causal factors that affect variations in native-speaker vocabulary size and these are represented in Figure 7.1 by the three boxes labelled social and personal factors, life experience, and opportunities for input and use. These in their turn affect the conditions for learning.

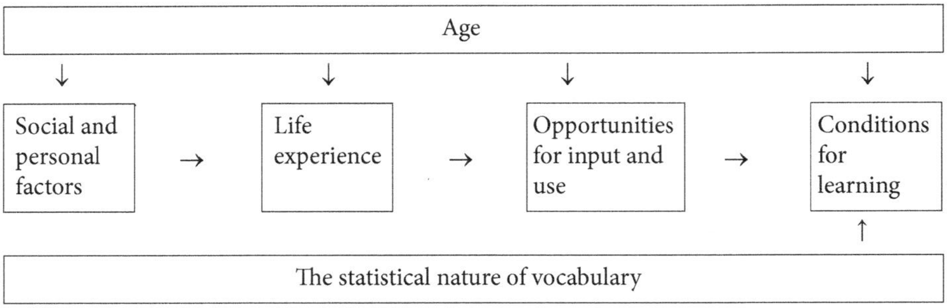

Figure 7.1 A model of factors affecting vocabulary size and growth

In the rest of this chapter, we will look at each of the parts of the model, explaining what each part represents and drawing on research to show the effect of each part on vocabulary size and growth. We will begin by looking at the two major factors affecting the rate at which a native-speaker's vocabulary grows.

Age and the statistical nature of vocabulary

Age

As we get older our vocabulary size grows, even into old age (Verhaeghen, 2003). A five-year-old has a larger vocabulary size than a three-year old. A teen-ager has a larger vocabulary size than a five-year old. A twenty-year-old will have a larger vocabulary size than they did when they were thirteen. The test takers in their 60s and older in the Coxhead, Nation, & Sim (2014) study scored the highest on the Vocabulary Size Test. Unfortunate health conditions can result in exceptions to this rule, but typically as native-speakers get older, they keep adding to the store of words that they know. Older native-speakers may have difficulty in accessing this store, but if meaning-recognition tests are used, the knowledge can usually be found. In very old age however (over 90-years-old), there may be a decline in vocabulary knowledge (Singer, Verhaeghen, Ghisletta, Lindenberger, & Baltes, 2003).

In a massive study of native-speakers of Dutch aged from 12 to 72 years old, Keuleers, Stevens, Mandera, and Brysbaert (2015) found that age was by far the most important predictor of vocabulary size among the variables they looked at, clearly showing that vocabulary size increases with age. This is not surprising, because increasing age results in cumulatively more contact with the language, and more contact with the language provides more opportunity to satisfy the vocabulary learning conditions of meeting new words and gaining repetitions of partly familiar words. These repetitions also provide opportunities for good quality conditions of noticing, retrieval, varied meetings and varied use, and elaboration to occur. Note in Figure 7.1 that age is related to each of the sets of factors affecting variability in vocabulary growth (signalled by the down-pointing arrows). Age affects social and personal factors such as our financial circumstances, cultural factors, family factors and personal interests, attitudes and motivation. Age also affects life experience factors such as the opportunity to travel, access to education, access to books, job choice, and interaction with others. Age also affects the quantity and quality of opportunities to use the language both receptively and productively.

The statistical nature of vocabulary

Vocabulary size does not grow at an even rate throughout life because there is a very important factor that both supports and limits vocabulary growth. In Figure 7.1, this is called the statistical nature of vocabulary. If we take an example of language use such as the text of this book, we can run the text through a computer program that lists the different words in the text and counts how often each word occurs. The resulting list of words shows us some interesting things about the statistical nature of language. Firstly, words occur with different frequencies. Some words like *the, of, same*, and *make* occur very often. The ten most frequent words of English account for around 25% of the different words on a page, the 100 most frequent words account for around 50% of the words on a page, and the one thousand most frequent words account for between 75% and 90% of the words on a page. A relatively small number of different words accounts for a very large proportion of the running words (the tokens) in a spoken or written text. Around 165 word families are function words (Nation, 2013, p. 23) and these by themselves can cover close to 50% of the running words in a text and have a marked effect on the coverage by the first 1000 words.

Another surprising feature is that in any normal text around half of the different words in the text occur only once. Even if the text is millions of running words long, around half of the different words will occur only once.

There is a law describing this statistical distribution of words called Zipf's Law. For a very readable description of Zipf's Law see Sorell (2012). It is also discussed in Nation (2013 Chapter 1). There is a closely related law called Herdan's Law (Herdan, 1960; Keuleers, Stevens, Mandera, & Brysbaert, 2015) which says that as we continue to meet more language in reading or listening, the rate of meeting new words will become lower. When we are in the early stages of learning our first language, we meet lots of new words. As the years pass and our vocabulary size increases, the chances of meeting new words become lower and lower. Because we need to meet new words and usually need to meet them repeatedly to have a chance of learning them, our opportunities for learning new words become fewer as we get older.

Figure 7.2 is taken from Keuleers, Stevens, Mandera & Brysbaert, (2015 p. 1675) and shows the slow-down in native-speaker vocabulary growth across the age groups in their study. The score on the vertical axis of the graph refers to a score out of 100 on a Yes/No vocabulary size test.

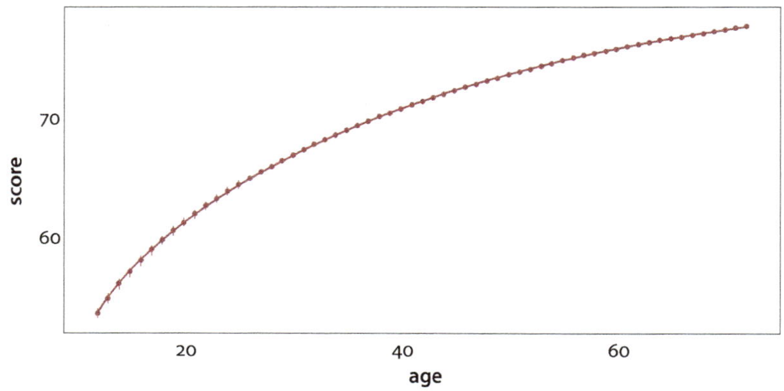

Figure 7.2 Vocabulary size across different age groups

The shape of the curve in Figure 7.2 is a very similar shape to that which would be predicted by Herdan's Law. Keuleers et al. (2015 p. 1685) concluded "the slowing of vocabulary growth with age is not linked to a decreasing capacity to learn new words but is the result of the ever smaller probability of encountering an unlearned word in the environment." Note that the vertical axis for the graph in Figure 7.2 does not start at zero and so does not show the rapid increase to the age of around 15-years-old which is very steep and slows after that. In the secondary school data from Coxhead, Nation, & Sim (2015), it appeared that Vocabulary Size Test scores increased more sharply in years when major national assessments began, typically in the third year of study at high school. It could be that there are times of learning when a threshold for vocabulary pushes knowledge along at a faster rate at some points in our lives. See Coxhead, McLaughlin, & Reid (2019) for more on thresholds in relation to learning technical vocabulary in trades education.

The statistical nature of vocabulary has positive effects on learning for at least the first twelve and possibly twenty years of life because the high-frequency and mid-frequency words of the language (Schmitt & Schmitt, 2014; Nation, 2013) are met so often and in such a varied range of circumstances that it would be difficult not to learn them. In studies of learning English as a foreign language, a distinction is made between high-frequency, mid-frequency and low-frequency words. The high-frequency words number around 3,000 and account for around 95% of the running words in most spoken and written uses of the language. The mid-frequency words add another 6,000 words and bring the total of high-frequency and mid-frequency words to 9,000 words. The rest of English vocabulary is classified as low-frequency words, although what may be seen as low-frequency words for many users of the language may in fact be very important and frequent for users with special interests or specialised occupations. Even native-speakers of English who are not truly literate learn most of the high-frequency and mid-frequency words by the time they are in the early years of secondary school, around the ages of 12 to14, having learned them through listening, viewing (watching TV and movies), and spoken interaction.

Age and the statistical nature of vocabulary determine the average rate at which a native-speaker's vocabulary grows. However, as we have seen, individuals' rates of growth can vary a lot and this variation between individuals is determined by the series of sets of factors in the central row of Figure 7.1, beginning with social and personal factors. Hoff (2006) provides an excellent comprehensive review of the factors affecting variations in vocabulary development.

Factors affecting variation between individuals in their rate of vocabulary growth

Before looking at each of the sets of factors in detail, let us look briefly at two examples of how they affect each other. The descriptions in brackets refer to parts of Figure 7.1. These examples will be looked at again later in this chapter with supporting references to the research.

It is a common finding in research on young native-speakers that children from high socio-economic groups perform better on measures of vocabulary knowledge than children from low socio-economic groups (social and personal factors). Researchers have related this to the way parents and care-givers interact with their children (life experience factors). Researchers then quantify the vocabulary aspect of the interaction by measuring the number of running words and different words that children hear and use (opportunities for input and use), on the assumption that quantity and quality of language met and used will affect vocabulary learning (conditions for learning). Some studies include a measure of vocabulary knowledge to show the relationship between amount of input and vocabulary knowledge.

Here is another example. In studies involving the vocabulary size of adults, level of education is a significant factor. Economic factors, cultural factors and personal factors (social and personal factors) all affect the amount and level of education an individual will experience (life experience factors). Higher education directly affects the quantity and variety of vocabulary that individuals will meet and the quality of the meetings with that vocabulary (opportunities for input and use). These varied and challenging interactions with academic and technical vocabulary provide very favourable conditions for vocabulary learning (conditions for learning).

There are many possible chains of cause and effect similar to the ones described in the two examples above and we will look at several more of them in this chapter.

The value of seeing a particular factor as a part of a model is that it provides a broader perspective that allows us to evaluate research focuses and interventions to increase vocabulary size involving that factor. For example, if we see a focus on extensive reading as a way of supporting young native-speakers' vocabulary growth opportunities for input and use, we should consider how this would affect the conditions for learning and what we would need to do to optimise these conditions. We should also consider which life experience factors and social and personal factors we would need to take account of to make the extensive reading program a success. This could include considering parental attitudes to reading, time available outside school to do the reading, and the children's motivation to read.

Let us now look in more detail at the first three sets of factors in the middle row of Figure 7.1 – social and personal factors, life experience factors, and opportunities for input and use. We have already looked at the fourth set of factors, learning conditions, at the beginning of this chapter.

Social and personal factors

Social and personal factors include economic factors, cultural factors, family factors, and personal factors.

Economic factors involve the amount of income that an individual or family has. This factor is often related to the factor of ethnicity, because there are often striking differences between the income of different racial groups. Children from low income groups and in schools in low income areas tend to have smaller vocabulary sizes than children in higher income areas (Hart & Risley, 1995; Farkas & Beron, 2004; Hoff, 2013).

Cultural factors include ethnicity (Farkas & Beron, 2004), social class (Hoff, 2006), attitudes to education, approaches to child-rearing (Hoff, 2006; Mastin & Vogt, 2016), amount of speech directed to children (Huttenlocher, Haight, Bryk, Seltzer, & Lyons, 1991; Fernald, Marchman, & Weisleder, 2013; Weisleder & Fernald, 2013; Golinkoff, Hoff, Rowe, Tamis-LeMonda, & Hirsh-Pasek, 2019), overheard speech (Sperry, Sperry, & Miller, 2019a; Brown & Gaskins, 2014), use of gesture (Rowe & Goldin-Meadow, 2009), quality of childcare, the significance of reading, and exposure to other languages. The amount of speech directed at young children has been shown to have a strong and enduring effect on vocabulary growth. Overheard speech, that is, speech not directed at children but which they can hear, also has an effect on vocabulary growth, and Sperry, Sperry, and Miller (2019b) argue strongly for its consideration in studies measuring amount of language input. Exposure to other related languages increases vocabulary size in the first language (Keuleers et al., 2015).

Family factors include family size, mother's level of education (Hoff, 2013), mother's age, and birth order. More educated parents are likely to know about good child-rearing practices, are more likely to use a richer vocabulary when talking to their children, and are more likely to seek the guidance of professionals or read about parenting issues. More educated parents are more likely to see learning as involving interaction rather than direct teaching, and to see a child's ability as a factor that can be changed and developed.

Personal factors include genes (Grasby, Coventry, Byrne, & Olson, 2019; Gathercole & Baddeley, 1993), gender (Huttenlocher, Haight, Bryk, Seltzer, & Lyons, 1991), interests, and attitude to school. Genes include size of working memory. Gathercole and Baddeley (1993) found that the capacity of the phonological loop predicted vocabulary size several years later for young native-speakers, with the effect becoming weaker as children got older and found ways to compensate for their phonological loop capacity. Grasby et al. (2019) looked at the effects of socio-economic status and genes on literacy and numeracy in a very large study involving twins in Australia. In studies in other countries, it has been found that high socio-economic status enhances genetic influences, and low socio-economic status enhances environmental influences. Their Australian data found that the influence of genetics and the environment on literacy and numeracy were largely the same across different socio-economic groups. Huttenlocher et al. (1991) found that young girls learned vocabulary at a faster rate than young boys.

Life experience factors

Life experience factors include (1) the amount and quality of interaction with family and others, (2) the amount and level of education, (3) habits of language use such as reading, viewing, oral interaction and writing, (4) hobbies and interests, (5) work, and (6) knowledge of other languages.

The amount and quality of interaction with family and others is included in what researchers call "parental skills". Farkas and Beron (2004) note that "the emerging synthesis among researchers [is that] parental skills and habits are the link between parental socio-economic background and the cognitive school success of their children. These skills and habits, rather than parental income per se, provide the causal mechanisms underlying the lower life achievement of low-income and ethnic minority children." (p. 471). Rowe (2018) provides a very clear and concise explanation of the link between socio-economic status and the amount and quality of interaction between parent and child. Hoff and Naigles (2002 p. 423) note that "Research findings suggest that the degree to which mother and child are mutually engaged in their conversations as well as the data provided in the utterances that mothers produce in conversation are related to children's lexical development."

Shneidman, Arroyo, Goldin-Meadow, and Levine (2013) found that children with multiple care-givers increased their vocabulary size through learning from all care-givers rather than just the parent. Similarly, the quality of teacher-talk in pre-school affects vocabulary knowledge several years later (Dickinson & Porche, 2011). Keuleers et al. (2015) found that level of education (Primary, Secondary, Bachelors, Masters) was related to vocabulary growth with higher levels of education relating to larger vocabulary sizes. For adults, education was a very influential factor.

Opportunities for input and use

Because vocabulary learning requires the conditions of spaced repetition, noticing, retrieval, varied meetings and use, and elaboration to occur, there need to be plenty of opportunities for language input and language use. The amount of spoken interaction between the parent and the child is very important in the vocabulary growth of very young children (Hart & Risley, 1995; Huttenlocher et al., 1991; Hurtado, Marchman, & Fernald, 2008; Fernald et al., 2013; Shneidman, Arroyo, Goldin-Meadow, & Levine, 2013). The amount and quality of this interaction is increased when a parent and a child read a book together (Dowdall et al., 2020), and this shared reading activity has positive effects on children's productive vocabulary growth (Senechal, Pagan, Lever, & Ouellette, 2008). The activity is most suited to two to three-year olds (Mol, Bus, de Jong & Smeets, 2008), but it is also a productive activity in primary school classes.

When care-givers use a diverse and sophisticated vocabulary, this contributes to young children's vocabulary growth (Hoff & Naigles, 2002; Pan, Rowe, Singer, & Snow, 2005; Rowe, 2012). Jones and Rowland (2017) found that variety (diversity) of vocabulary input may be a more crucial factor for children's vocabulary growth than sheer quantity of input.

Research by Sutarsyah, Nation, and Kennedy (1994) showed that diversity of topic results in a very substantial increase in the number of different words used compared with the same length of text on a single topic by one writer, and education increases the opportunity to deal in depth with a wide range of various topics.

Some well-researched causal chains

We have now looked at the four sets of causally related factors in the middle row of Figure 7.1 that affect the rate of vocabulary growth – social and personal factors, life experience factors, opportunities for input and use, and conditions for learning. These factors are part of causal chains, and in this section we look at five examples of causal chains affecting the vocabulary size of native-speakers. These chains involve (1) the 30-million-word gap, (2) the role of education, (3) parenting skills, (4) guessing from context, and (5) knowledge of other languages. These particular chains have been chosen because of their importance in vocabulary size and growth and because they emphasize factors at different parts of the causal chains. For example, the 30-million-word gap has its root in socio-economic factors. Education and parenting skills are very much life experience factors. Guessing the meanings of words from context is an amount of input and use factor. Although a part of the chain is emphasised with each of these examples, each one is nonetheless involved in a causal chain. For an excellent example of an explanation of a causal chain between socio-economic status and the vocabulary gap, see Rowe (2018).

The 30-million-word gap

The most highly publicized factor affecting the vocabulary growth of very young native-speakers is referred to as "the 30-million-word gap" originating from the research of Hart and Risley (1995). As a result of their research, Hart and Risley claimed that children in low socio-economic homes heard 30-million running words fewer than children in economically better-off homes. The children who were the focus of the study were from 10 months to 36 months old. The study received a lot of praise from academics (the first four pages of the book consist of laudatory comments) and wide attention from the media.

The causal chain was that parents in low socio-economic families have poor parenting skills which result in much less parent-child interaction and thus less spoken input directed to the child than there should be, as much 30-million-words less over a period of just over two years. As a result, children in low socio-economic families have fewer opportunities to learn new words and so have smaller vocabulary sizes than children in higher socio-economic families who receive much more input. Note that this argument is purely a quantity-based argument. Hart and Risley found no major differences in the quality (richness) of the language that parents and children in low socio-economic status families produced. Hart and Risley looked at the quality of interaction in order to find examples of how interaction can help learning. If there is more of this helpful interaction, then there will be presumably more learning. They note "All the quality features of language and interaction were present in the everyday parenting that all children experienced *but in differing amounts*" (p. 112, italics added). "The richness of quality features in parents' utterances hardly varied. Whether a parent talked a lot or a little, such quality features as different words, questions, clauses, past-tense verbs, and affirmatives and prohibitions occurred approximately equally often per parent utterance." (pp. 127–8). Their argument about quality of interaction therefore still remains a quantity argument. That is, if lower socio-economic status parents did more of what they already do, it would be much better for the children.

Various studies that use a vocabulary measure, like the Peabody Picture Vocabulary Test or the Looking-while-Listening procedure show a persistent vocabulary knowledge gap between children from high and low socio-economic households (Farkas & Beron, 2004; Hoff, 2006; Weisleder & Fernald, 2013). Farkas and Beron (2004) using the Peabody Picture Vocabulary Test found significant vocabulary gaps between Black and White children, and between children of different socio-economic groups, for children as young as 36 months. By the time children were five years old, the gap was at the size at which it stayed for at least the next eight years, with Black children between one year or two years behind White children in their vocabulary score. If the vocabulary growth rates of the early output studies and Biemiller and Slonim's studies are applied to these results, then a gap of one to two years would be a gap of 1000 to 2000 word families for learners aged five and above.

A striking finding by Farkas and Beron is that the rate of increase on the Peabody Picture Vocabulary Test scores remains the same between Black and White children after they enter school, but the gap in the scores that existed before then persists. That is, both Black and White children acquire vocabulary at roughly the same rate during their school years, but the gap in vocabulary size that existed before then is not closed. To close the gap, Black children would have to learn vocabulary at a faster rate than White children.

The role of education

The second example of a causal chain that we will look at focuses on the role of education in vocabulary growth. For adults, Keuleers, Stevens, Mandera, and Brysbaert (2015) found a strong relationship between levels of education and vocabulary size. In their study, education was a four-level category – (1) no education/primary school, (2) secondary school, (3) Bachelor's degree, and (4) Master's degree. The largest vocabulary size increase occurred between secondary and Bachelor level education, and the next largest between Bachelor's and Master's. Social and personal factors can affect access to education and the valuing of higher education. Education is a life experience factor, and university education involves the detailed study of a major subject and a variety of minor subjects. Each subject has its own technical vocabulary of a thousand or more words, and the study of each subject involves meeting and using the subject matter vocabulary in a considered way across the range of language skills of listening, speaking, reading and writing. Education thus provides plenty of opportunities for language input and language use and sets up ideal conditions for vocabulary learning. It is thus not surprising that education has a major effect on vocabulary growth.

Parental skills and habits

Parental skills and habits fit into life experience factors in Figure 7.1 and are seen to involve cognitive stimulation within the home. Researchers see parental skills and habits as being directly affected by the social and personal factors of socio-economic status and education. Parental skills and habits directly affect the amount of input and the amount of quality input that children receive. The cognitive stimulation gained from skilled parental input, particularly from a vocabulary perspective, needs to be seen broadly because vocabulary is learned (1) through repeated meetings with words and (2) through the quality of those encounters. Meetings and repeated meetings occur through quantity and variety of input such as talking and doing things with family members and friends, watching television and movies, reading and being read to, playing with peers, gaining experience beyond the home through going to day care centres, and going on holidays and journeys to a variety of places. The quality of encounters with words is enriched through talk directed to the child, through challenging discussion and description where particular words re-occur in a variety of contexts, through engaging in reading around a topic where words have a chance to re-occur, through putting words to use in speaking and writing which stretches knowledge, and through deliberately focusing on words in a range of ways that develops skills in attending to the form, meaning and use of words (Weisleder & Fernald, 2013). Research suggests that for young children at least, "eavesdropping" is not a major source of vocabulary learning. Children benefit most from talk that directly engages them and is directed towards them (Huttenlocher et al., 1991; Rowe, 2012; Shneidman et al., 2013). Parental skills are involved in setting up and directly providing these opportunities (Cartmill et al., 2013).

Guessing the meanings of words from context

In our fourth of the five examples of causal chains affecting vocabulary growth, we look at the skill of inferring the meanings of words from context clues. Most of the vocabulary learning by native-speakers of English occurs incidentally as a part of normal receptive and productive communication. When children can read, then guessing from context while reading can be a major means of vocabulary growth. Although this seems obvious, it was difficult to prove experimentally until Nagy, Herman and Anderson (1985) showed, by using sensitive vocabulary tests that could tap partial knowledge of words, "small but statistically reliable gains in word knowledge from context" (p. 233). By combining data from their study with estimates of the amount of reading done by middle grade children, they estimated that "the number of new words the typical middle grade child learns in a year from context during reading is between 750 and 5,500; the point value estimate is 3,125" (p. 250). The amount of learning would depend on the amount of reading. The causal chain here is that attitude and engagement with school results in skill in reading. Skill in reading coupled with skill in guessing word meanings from context can result in substantial amounts of reading and substantial vocabulary learning. In the early stages of reading, the amount of vocabulary learning could be affected by genetic differences in the size of working memory which could affect guessing from context. As children get older however, the size of working memory plays less of a role in vocabulary learning (Gathercole & Baddeley, 1993).

The effect of learning additional languages

Keuleers, Stevens, Mandera, and Brysbaert (2015), while researching a test of Dutch vocabulary size, found that knowledge of other languages had a positive effect on L1 vocabulary size – "... the vocabulary that multilinguals acquire in related languages seems to increase their first language (L1) vocabulary size and outweighs the loss caused by decreased exposure to L1." (Keuleers et al., 2015 p. 1665). They considered that a major reason for this was that knowledge of other languages supported knowledge of cognate or loan words in the L1. The causal chain here is that the cultural factor of exposure to other languages leads to the life experience factor of gaining knowledge of other languages and this leads to the opportunity for input factor of knowledge of cognate words or loan words making it easier to learn the related words in English.

The total multilingual vocabulary for a person who is exposed to multiple languages could be larger than the total vocabulary of an L1 speaker with same amount of total exposure. Adding to this, the more that foreign language exposure leads to shared vocabulary with L1, the less that decreased L1 exposure will impact vocabulary size. This would be particularly true for closely related languages like English and Dutch, but it is also possible that people who know languages that have a lot of recent borrowing from English such as Japanese (Daulton, 2008) could benefit from this knowledge.

The PVST and the VST do not measure knowledge of words from languages other than English which have not yet become part of English. This omission is most serious for speakers of heritage languages such as Maori in New Zealand and for the children of recent immigrants to a country such as Samoans, Cook Islanders, Tongans, Chinese or Somali in New Zealand. Such children may know a large number of words that reflect their knowledge of the cultural experiences gained from their participation in their parents' culture. This vocabulary knowledge is properly considered as part of their total vocabulary size in a roughly similar way to which knowledge of the vocabulary of specialist areas is properly considered part of a person's vocabulary size. A person need not be a native-speaker of another language or even need not be fluent in that language in order to know a substantial number of words from that language. Although this knowledge of other languages is not a part of English vocabulary size, it is certainly a part of an individual's total vocabulary size.

Although specialised areas of vocabulary knowledge may not seem to be core to the vocabulary of a language, to each user with that knowledge it is undoubtedly an important part of their vocabulary and is core to their interests. This may be most obvious with vocabulary related to religion where religious practice and experience is reflected in its accompanying vocabulary. Different religions and different religious denominations follow different practices, and while the related vocabulary may be of little use to someone of a different religion or of no religion, it is central to the lives of those who follow that religion. Vocabulary from other languages may work in a similar way. For those with close connections to that language community, that vocabulary is central to their lives. For those with few or no connections, it is not central.

Measuring this knowledge requires other tests than tests such as the PVST or VST. If other tests are not used, then any measure of such learners' vocabulary size will obviously be an underestimate. The failure to develop such tests may also show an undervaluing of the contribution of those other languages.

An overview of factors affecting vocabulary size and growth

The model in Figure 7.1 can be expressed as a set of principles. These principles provide a useful summary for this chapter.

1. Vocabulary learning occurs as a result of the quantity and quality of vocabulary input and use.
2. The quantity and quality of input and use is affected by the amount and variety of opportunities to meet and use the language.
3. The opportunities for input and use are affected by the life experience factors of (1) interaction with family and others, (2) the amount and level of education, (3) habits of language use such as reading, viewing, oral interaction and writing, (4) hobbies and interests, (5) work, and (6) knowledge of other languages.
4. Life experience factors are affected by social and personal factors such as economic factors, cultural factors, family factors and personal factors.
5. Vocabulary size increases with age because time provides cumulatively increasing opportunities for the conditions of quantity and quality of vocabulary input and use to occur.
6. The statistical nature of vocabulary results in an eventual slowing of the rate of vocabulary growth as there are fewer and fewer opportunities meet new words and to meet partly familiar words often enough to learn them.
7. Age and the statistical nature of vocabulary determine the average rate of vocabulary growth. Chains of a wide range of other factors determine individual variability in vocabulary size.

In the following chapter, we build on the ideas in this chapter to examine how native-speakers of various ages can be supported to increase their vocabulary size.

CHAPTER 8

Supporting native-speaker vocabulary growth

In this chapter we look at how parents, teachers and individuals themselves can support vocabulary growth. The chapter is organized around the age and education levels of (1) toddlers and pre-school, (2) primary school, (3) secondary school, and (4) adults. In essence, supporting vocabulary size growth involves providing large quantities of varied input that involves good quality encounters with vocabulary. Most native-speaker learning of vocabulary occurs incidentally when learners are focused on using the language to communicate. As learners become older, the opportunities for a deliberate focus on vocabulary and vocabulary learning increase, and it is worth making use of these opportunities in a planned and informed way. However, the deliberate learning of vocabulary can only be a supplement to large quantities of rich and varied use of the language through the four skills of listening, speaking, reading and writing.

Toddlers and pre-school

The critical factor in vocabulary size growth in very young children is the amount and variety of interaction between the primary care-giver and the child. As we have seen in Chapter 7, the amount and variety of this interaction can be constrained by socio-economic factors. Addressing the related socio-economic factors of income, parents' education and employment would be an excellent start to improving vocabulary size growth. Other interventions such as parent training in child-rearing and in interacting with children, television programs for young children, and supporting child-care centres may be effective, but are one step away from the basic causes of variation in native-speaker vocabulary size growth. Nevertheless, such interventions are worthwhile, and we will look at the research on them here.

Parent training in interacting with children

Parents can benefit from training in how to interact with their children in ways that affect the linguistic and interactional features of their language use (Suskind et al., 2016), although making a change which persists is difficult. Improving linguistic features involves using fewer directives, using more questions, using challenges, and making use of a more diverse vocabulary. Improving interactional features involves more commenting on actions as they take place and engaging in back and forth conversation. Setting up interactional cycles during shared reading or when responding to questions increases the quantity and quality of interaction (Deckner et al., 2006). The parents' input encourages children to speak, and children's questions and comments can influence parents' input. These interactional cycles are encouraged when parents give causal explanations to children's questions.

Shared picture-book reading provides opportunities for quality interaction because picture books for children contain many features that support vocabulary growth. Besides being interesting and engaging, picture books incorporate informal vocabulary control ensuring that the language of the book will be largely familiar to children. They use pictures that illustrate and enrich words in the text and that provide a basis for interaction between the child and the parent reading the text to the child. They also provide repetition of vocabulary and sentences, often with small changes setting up useful conditions for vocabulary learning. These features of the book are greatly enhanced when a parent reading the book to a child interacts with the child about the book. Dowdall et al. (2020) conducted a meta-analysis of studies of interventions involving training in shared-book reading. They found that training adults in shared-book reading greatly improved their skill in using the technique regardless of the level of education of the care-giver. They also found small-sized effects on both productive and receptive vocabulary knowledge. Shared-reading is a useful technique for improving the quality of parent-child interaction, and if it is done often enough will have positive effects on vocabulary growth.

Training parents in ways of interacting with their children should also have the goal of enriching parents' views of the nature of learning, of the value of using a rich vocabulary, of the value of spending time with a child, and of the ability of a child to change with help. Learning and vocabulary growth do not necessarily require teaching, but they do require interaction and the enrichment of experience.

Experiencing and talking about the world

Willard et al. (2019) looked at parent-child interactions at a museum exhibit, looking at how a range of different prompts (encouragement to explain, encouragement to explore, questions) and behaviour (parent explanation) affected parent-child interactions. They found that these small interventions had noticeable positive effects on parent-child interaction. Although the study did not examine the vocabulary involved in the interactions, it is not hard to see that getting children to explore and explain is likely to result in vocabulary use that requires the use of relevant topic-related vocabulary and stretches the use of partly known vocabulary. The richness of parent-child interactions is likely to be accompanied by a richness of vocabulary use.

Doing lots of different things

Providing diversity of experience is a critical factor in increasing vocabulary size (Jones & Rowland, 2017). This diversity of experience needs to be accompanied by interaction between the care-giver and the child so that the new vocabulary related to the experience occurs, is repeated, and gets some attention.

These experiences can include going to parks and playgrounds, going swimming, going to the church, temple or mosque, going to the library, going to the zoo, going on a train or bus, going to a friend's house, going to a cultural celebration such as a wedding or birthday party, playing new games, going to a movie theatre, going to a parade, going to a museum or art gallery, and going to the mall.

Each experience can be talked about several times – while having the experience and after coming home, including talking about a future visit to the same place. It can also include reporting the experience to another family member or friend.

Getting ready for learning to read

Parents can help young children get ready for reading through the interactive reading of picture books (shared-book reading), through reading to children, through helping children learn about books, through the playing of games which develop phonemic awareness, and through a gradual introduction to the alphabetic principle.

Learning about books involves getting familiar with the basic conventions of knowing that books contain stories and information, that the printed words in a book convey information and have spoken forms, that you start at the beginning of the book and move through to the end, that English print goes across the page, and that lines of print step down the page. Learning about books also involves learning how pictures relate to the story. This knowledge does not involve direct teaching but develops through the interactive use of books.

A very helpful way of getting young children ready for reading an alphabetic language such as English is to develop their phonemic awareness. Phonemic awareness is the realization that sounds go together to make words and that words can be broken down into separate sounds. The following game is a good way to develop phonemic awareness. "What word is this? C a t?" When sounding out the word the parent does not say the names of the letters (see aye tee) but says the sound of the letters (/k æ t/). The child has to work out that these three sounds go together to make the sound of the word *cat*. Parents should play this game often with their children and when the child gets good at doing it, they can then get the child to test the parent by making the sounds so the parent has to guess the word. Phonemic awareness is excellent preparation for reading, but some children may not be ready to play such games until they are five or six years old.

The alphabetic principle involves the realization that letters can represent sounds. Children can be helped with learning this by getting them to look for the letter *p* for example on a page and being told what sound it signals. Although English has many irregularities in sound-spelling correspondences, the regularities far outnumber the irregularities (Nation & Macalister, 2021 Appendix 1).

Knowing about books, phonemic awareness, and familiarity with the alphabetic principle, all prepare a child well for beginning to read.

Primary school

The main focuses of vocabulary growth at primary school should be through the collaborative spoken engagement with new ideas and new ways of discovering about the world, and through reading. At primary school, learners should also be introduced to the more formal study of vocabulary and should begin to develop *word consciousness*.

Vocabulary learning through oral interaction

Oral interaction in the classroom is an important means of vocabulary growth, particularly if the interaction involves learners in exploring new areas of knowledge. Vocabulary learning is enhanced if some deliberate attention (Elley, 1989) is given to the vocabulary in the interaction. This deliberate attention can be simply writing the word on the board or giving some brief attention to its meaning. What is most important however is that the children have opportunities to interact with the teacher and with each other about the content of the lesson and have plenty of opportunities to hear and use the related vocabulary. Such interaction can also occur around multimedia resources.

Vocabulary learning through reading

Ideally, learning to read should be a continuation of home and pre-school-based activities like the interactive reading of picture books, being read to, the playing of games which develop phonemic awareness, and a gradual introduction to the alphabetic principle. The goal of learning to read should involve getting learners excited about reading and developing a love of reading, along with developing confidence in their ability to read and to use reading to learn new ideas.

It has been suggested that the relationship between reading and vocabulary growth changes as children learn to read (Chall, 1987). Initially, learning to read involves working with known vocabulary so that vocabulary knowledge developed through spoken interaction supports reading. As control of the reading skill develops, reading increasingly involves meeting new ideas and the vocabulary that conveys them. The focus then gradually moves from vocabulary supporting reading to reading supporting vocabulary growth. This change of focus is probably most noticeable in upper primary school when children's vocabulary size moves beyond the most frequent six or seven-thousand word families of spoken language at around the ages of eight or nine-years-old into the more formal vocabulary of written text. In vocabulary frequency counts, the mid-frequency vocabulary ends at around 9,000 word families (Schmitt & Schmitt, 2014; Nation, 2013, Chapter 1). This roughly is when learners are getting ready to move from primary school to secondary school and already have a good control of the vocabulary needed for spoken interaction.

A good school system ensures that each child learns to read, that there is monitoring that identifies those who are struggling to read, and that there are reading recovery programs that support those who struggle with reading.

A well-balanced reading program should include large amounts of independent reading (extensive reading), intensive reading where learners read challenging texts with support, and reading for fluency where learners read easy material with some pressure to go faster. Reading contributes to vocabulary growth by increasing the speed of access to familiar words, by strengthening and enriching partly known words through repeated, varied meetings, and by introducing learners to unknown words in meaningful contexts. The quantity of varied extensive reading is directly linked to growth in vocabulary size (Nagy, Herman, & Anderson, 1985).

Shared reading has positive effects on learning to read and vocabulary growth (Pollard-Durodolla et al., 2011). It can be viewed as a kind of intensive reading where the teacher provides support during the reading through interaction with the children.

The deliberate teaching and learning of vocabulary

Some researchers advocate the deliberate teaching of vocabulary as a way of bridging the vocabulary gap (Duff & Brydon, 2020). Teachers need to become familiar with word frequency lists, particularly the high frequency and the mid-frequency vocabulary which comprise the most frequent 9,000 words of English. Teachers need to be able to relate learners' vocabulary size test scores to these lists so that in deliberate teaching there is a focus on vocabulary that is at the margins of the learners' vocabulary knowledge. Teachers tend to underestimate how many words learners know and in the absence of test data they should at least assume that the rough rule of thumb of age minus two times 1000 represents their learners' current vocabulary knowledge.

The teacher should make use of the techniques of a Word Wall, Word Experts, a vocabulary box for peer testing, and rich instruction of vocabulary to focus on somewhere between 3 to 5 words a day, every school day, as well as coming back to vocabulary previously focused on.

A Word Wall is simply made up of lots of cards pinned to the wall. Each word is written on a card and its meaning is written on another card of a different colour. A number in the form of the date (20210411 – year month day) is written on the back of each card so that they can be matched. As words occur during class activities they are added to the Word Wall. They can be words from the topics that the learners are studying. They can be words that exemplify important spelling rules. They can be words that have occurred in intensive reading or class discussion. The teacher involves the learners in activities using the cards on the Word Wall. These can include matching words and their meanings, recalling meanings when the word forms are presented, and recalling word forms when meanings are presented. Individual learners can choose items from the Word Wall to use in the Word Experts activity.

The Word Experts activity involves a learner choosing a word that interests them and then gathering information about the word to present to others in the class or to the whole class. The word should initially be met in language use so that the learner has a sentence context to support the search for information on the word. The activity has three goals – (1) to get the learners learning new words, (2) to make learners aware of what is involved in knowing a word, and (3) to train learners in finding information about words. Knowing a word involves knowing its form (spoken, written, word parts), knowing its meaning (its core meaning, its senses, and its associations), and knowing its function (its part of speech, the grammatical patterns it can fit into, its collocations, and constraints on its use) (Nation, 2013, Chapter 2). The teacher working with the learners can prepare an increasingly elaborated template for them to use when gathering information about a word. The teacher should also make the learners aware of sources of information (dictionaries, concordancers, older language users) and guide them in web-based searches. Words from Word Expert presentations can be added to the Word Wall.

Having a class vocabulary box (Coxhead, 2004) is a way of keeping track of vocabulary that is encountered in class, raising learners' awareness of vocabulary, encouraging vocabulary learning individually and as a class, working on aspects of word knowledge, and building shared vocabulary knowledge for students and teachers. The purpose of a vocabulary box is to store word cards that the class develops during a course of study and use them for deliberate learning, revision activities and independent learning. A vocabulary box needs to be easily accessible so learners can easily get the word cards out of the box. A shoe box is about the right size.

The word cards are usually pieces of blank cardboard that are about 6 × 8 centimetres (about the size of a regular playing card). Word cards are very easy to use, and it is important that the cards are quite stiff and strong, because they get handled a lot by learners. Before making word cards, have learners first of all decide which words or expressions from class each day should go into the box. Learners can take responsibility for making at least two or three cards each per day, and in this way, the number of word cards builds quickly. It is important that learners understand how to make a word card and the principles behind learning words using word cards (see Nation, 2013, pp. 437–478; Coxhead, 2004).

To make a word card, on one side have the learners write the target word or phrase and information about the word, such as how it is pronounced, word grammar (e.g. noun, verb, adjective, and so on), or word stress. On the other side of the card, have the learners write the meaning of the word or a translation if the class members share the same first language, and perhaps an example of the word in a sentence. It can be helpful to use any context or sentence from the class that day, because it can help the learners associate the word with what they were learning about in class, at least initially. Because only one side of the card is visible at any one time, learners have to recall or retrieve the meaning of the words if they are looking at the target word side, or the form of the word if they are looking at the meaning side. This retrieval process strengthens learning. When they are writing word cards, learners can use learner dictionaries or their class texts or examples from class to help complete the cards. It is important that the cards get checked carefully. Other students can do this. Shared responsibility for the cards is important, and in our experience, students take this responsibility seriously. Once the cards are made and checked, they go into the vocabulary box.

The word cards are then available for everyone to use and the number of word cards can increase rapidly over time because more cards are made and checked every day. It might be helpful to use different coloured cards to keep track of words from week to week, for example. Cards can be used by individual class members for quiet revision, meaning learners just take a stack of cards from the box and work through their stack looking at one side, and trying to recall the meaning or form of the target item. Learners can also work in pairs or groups with words, testing each other on the meaning of the words, common collocations, word family members, first language translation, example sentences or as a memory game. As a class, the vocabulary box words can be used for regular quizzes, ranking activities or mind mapping with words in connection with topics or stories, creating gap fills, preparing talks, or writing activities. After a short amount of time, learners are usually able to say whether a word or expression is in the vocabulary box or needs to be added.

Learners find vocabulary boxes so useful that they may start their own box and word card set at home. Over the course of 12 weeks, for example, classes can create and use more than 800 word cards. This is a good amount of concentrated vocabulary learning and speaks to the power of word cards as a learning strategy.

Rich instruction involves the teacher spending time on a word in class. Such instruction can cover some of the aspects involved in knowing a word, and can be a kind of training for the Word Experts activity. Words dealt with in rich instruction should be words that are of value to the learners because they relate closely to topics covered in class or are generally very useful words. It is helpful if such instruction arises out of meeting the word in use. Words covered in rich instruction should go into the vocabulary box and should get some spaced, repeated attention.

Word consciousness

Word consciousness involves the deliberate awareness of words, their nature, and the jobs they do. For a detailed account of word consciousness see Chapter 9 of van Hees and Nation (2017). The term *word consciousness* was first used by Scott and Nagy (2004) and is a very useful way of bringing together a wide range of deliberate focuses on vocabulary. Here are some of the ideas that can be included in word consciousness.

1. A word can have a wide range of uses and these different uses usually share a core meaning. A useful way to explore this idea is to look at the meanings given for a word such as *sweet* in a dictionary and to work out what is common to all these meanings,
2. A dictionary is a rich and useful source of information about words. Looking carefully at an entry in a dictionary can begin to make learners aware of what is involved in knowing a word and how to get useful information from a dictionary.
3. Many English words have prefixes and suffixes, and these prefixes and suffixes have meanings that are part of the meaning of a word. Children can enjoy breaking words into word parts and seeing how the meanings of the parts relate to the meaning of the whole word. Children can also be introduced to the idea of word families. A word family is a word with all its closely related inflected and derived forms. Here is an example: *thirst, thirsted, thirstier, thirstiest, thirstily, thirstiness, thirsting, thirsts, thirsty.*

4. Some English words have a stem that can be found in other words and that has a similar meaning in those words. The stem *spect* for example can be found in words such as *inspect, spectacles* and *spectator* It is worth learning a small number of these very useful stems (Wei & Nation, 2013), because they can help in understanding and remembering words that contain them.
5. Words occur with other words to make up common phrases and sayings. Sometimes these phrases such as *put up with, in the nick of time, going forward, the light at the end of the tunnel, a piece of cake* and *sweet as* take on a special meaning. Learners can collect such phrases, do a little bit of research on them, and talk about them in class.
6. Some words have the same spoken form and written form but have completely different meanings, for example, *bowl* meaning a shape and *bowl* meaning to roll a ball. Some words sound the same but have different spellings and different meanings (*their* and *there*). Some have the same spelling but do not sound the same and have different meanings (*close* meaning "near" and *close* meaning "to shut"). Learners can be given some of these pairs and work out what is the same and different with each pair.
7. Knowing a word involves knowing a lot about a word – its spoken form, its written form, its family members, its word parts, its meaning, its part of speech, the other words it typically occurs with (its collocations), its synonyms and opposites, and any restrictions on its use such as whether it is a polite word or not, whether it is mainly used in the United States, whether it is an old-fashioned word and so on (Nation 2013, Chapter 2). Children can gather a lot of such information about a new word they have met and present this information to their classmates (the Word Experts activity).
8. Some words are much more commonly used than other words. Some words occur very rarely. By running a short text through a word counting program (try <https://www.lextutor.ca/freq/>), children learn something about word frequency and consider how these ideas about frequency could guide learning the vocabulary of another language and their learning of English. The most important ideas are (1) a small number of words are very common and cover a large percentage of the words in any text; (2) about half of the different words in a text, even a very long text, occur only once; (3) the most common words are usually very short words; (4) the less common words are usually long and have word parts.

There are other possible focuses for word consciousness activities, but the above list covers the most important. The challenge for the teacher is to present these focuses in age-appropriate ways so that the children can understand and learn from them.

Learning how to learn words

Even from a very young age, children need to learn how to learn. They need to be aware of and practise the very basic and powerful principles of learning. These include (1) the importance of repetition, (2) the importance of retrieval (recalling what you have studied), (3) the importance of spacing retrievals rather than massing them, (4) the value of using analysis and elaboration to make words stick in memory (adding quality to repetition), (5) the value of producing what you want to learn (saying it or writing it), (6) the need to balance the opportunities for learning across input, output, deliberate study and fluency development, and (7) the value of being able to find information without relying on a teacher. These principles apply very strongly to the learning of vocabulary, but they also apply to learning school subjects and learning outside school. The seven principles are strongly supported by research (see Macalister & Nation, 2020 for more detail on principles).

Guidelines for teachers for supporting primary school children's vocabulary growth

1. Make sure that in each school day there are opportunities for meaningful oral language exchanges and meaningful listening.
2. Develop clear reading goals with each learner and their family for reading at home, and also make sure that in each school day there is reading during class time.
3. In the early levels of primary school do shared reading and audio-supported reading.
4. Carefully monitor each learner's reading skill and diagnose any reading problems that they have. Find solutions to these problems. Test learners' vocabulary size using the Picture Vocabulary Size Test for learners seven-years old or younger and use part of the Vocabulary Size Test for older learners.
5. Use the data from vocabulary testing to guide the deliberate teaching of vocabulary supported by a word wall, a vocabulary box, and the Word Experts activity where learners research and describe words to their classmates. Aim at adding at least two or three words a day to the word wall or vocabulary box.
6. Systematically develop learners' word consciousness so that the children are excited and interested about learning new vocabulary.
7. Accompany word consciousness activities with sustained training in the principles of learning and their application to the learning of vocabulary.
8. Work with learners' families to make sure that school work is well supported and that learning goals are well understood.

See van Hees & Nation (2017, Chapter 10) for further information.

Secondary school

Vocabulary knowledge underlies the four skills of listening, speaking, reading and writing, and teachers of native-speakers of English at secondary school are often concerned that their learners' vocabulary knowledge may not be enough for the academic tasks they need to do. Teachers may also be concerned that some of their learners may be dealing with issues of English as a second language and this impacts on the success of their study. The suggestions in this section are largely directed to teachers at secondary school. However, parents can support the vocabulary growth of teen-agers by encouraging them to read a lot and to read widely, by encouraging hobbies and interests that will engage them in reading, writing and interaction with others, by providing opportunities to experience new fields of knowledge, and by engaging them in challenging discussion. Given the nature of teen-agers though, it is worth remembering Mark Twain's comment: "When I was a boy of 14, my father was so ignorant I could hardly stand to have the old man around. But when I got to be 21, I was astonished at how much the old man had learned in seven years."

Vocabulary size is of interest to those concerned with reading, because of the relationship between vocabulary size and the coverage of words in a text which affects comprehension. Table 8.1 shows that a vocabulary size of around 8000 word families is needed to get close to the desired 98% coverage of the running words in a Year 9 science text designed for the beginning of secondary school. Similar vocabulary sizes are needed to get this 98% coverage for novels, newspapers, and

Table 8.1 Cumulative percentage coverage figures for a Year 9 science text

Levels	Cumulative coverage*
1st 1000	82.93%
2nd 1000	90.14%
3rd 1000	93.28%
4th 1000	95.06%
5th 1000	96.13%
6th 1000	96.88%
7th 1000	97.43%
8th 1000	97.90%
9th 1000	98.22%
10th 1000	98.46%
11th 1000	98.67%
12th 1000	98.87%
13th 1000	98.98%
14th 1000	99.01%
Not in lists	100%

* including proper names

movies (Nation, 2006). 98% coverage means there is one unknown word in every 50, or one in every five lines, or six or seven unknown words per page. Knowing a learner's vocabulary size is a very useful step towards seeing if vocabulary size is a major factor in a learner's difficulties in reading.

Using the Vocabulary Size Test

In Chapter 5 we looked at the Vocabulary Size Test. Research with testing vocabulary size in New Zealand secondary schools (Coxhead, Nation, Woods, & Sim, 2018) has shown that around one-third of the learners sitting a group-administered test gain substantially lower scores than if the test is administered one-on-one with the administrator encouraging the learner to stay on task and helping with reading and format difficulties. The major reason for this is that in a group-administered test we cannot be sure if the learner is taking the test seriously. We also cannot be sure if there are other important factors, like reading skill, test taking strategy, attention span, familiarity with the format, and problems with the test itself, which are having a strong influence on the results of the test. Testing on a one-on-one basis can yield much more valid data than group testing because some of these factors can be observed and controlled for. Table 8.2 describes how to administer the test.

Table 8.2 Features involved in administering the *Vocabulary Size Test* and their effects

Features of testing	Effects
Individual testing (one-on-one)	Maintain attention
Explain the purpose of the test	Maintain motivation
Get the learner to read the items aloud if the learner seems to be having problems	Control for reading skill Make the learner consider all choices (test taking strategy)
Occasionally discuss items	Evaluate the test Consider test taking strategy
Break up testing with interviewing	Reduce fatigue Gather supporting data
Use only part of the test	Avoid fatigue Reduce testing time

As each item is answered, the administrator can say "Good" even if the answer is incorrect. In the very early parts of the test, particularly for the first ten or fifteen items, the learner can be questioned about a wrong answer. Learners at secondary school should definitely know all of the early words because they are among the most frequent words in the language. Wrong answers on these items indicate a problem with reading, motivation, attention, or test-taking strategy (not considering all choices), and these problems need to be dealt with early so they do not affect the rest of the test. In the later parts of the test, learners should try to answer each item unless they feel they know nothing about the word.

The vocabulary sizes of native-speakers in New Zealand secondary schools

The following observations are based largely on Coxhead, Nation, & Sim (2015).

1. Who is a native-speaker? If the learners were born in an English-speaking country, they are effectively native-speakers of English with regard to vocabulary size. If learners were not born in an English-speaking country, but came at a young age (before the age of nine or ten), they are soon likely to be native-speakers of English from a vocabulary perspective. That is their vocabulary size will soon be similar to learners born there.
2. The rough rule of thumb that one year of life equals 1000 word families seems to be true, especially if we start counting from two or three years old. Thus to work out what a learner's vocabulary size is likely to be, take their age in years, minus 2, times 1000. So, a thirteen year old is likely to have a vocabulary size around 11,000 words, and a seventeen year old around 15,000 words.
3. Most learners are within plus or minus 2000 words of this rule of thumb. A very small number of learners may be around plus or minus 4000 words either side of the rule of thumb.
4. Learners from low socio-economic backgrounds tend to be on the lower side of the rule of thumb, in effect one or two years lower than learners from a higher socio-economic background.
5. The amount of reading that learners do outside school varies a lot. Some learners always have a book on the go, others read magazines regularly, few read newspapers, and some do little reading at all outside of school.
6. The amount of reading that learners do typically affects their receptive vocabulary size.
7. A few learners may have severe reading problems which require diagnosis and one-on-one teaching. Nonetheless, their vocabulary sizes are still likely to roughly fit the rule of thumb (age minus 2 times 1000) because they will still pick up their vocabulary through listening.

Vocabulary size is a reflection of variety of experience. That is, the more varied the things learners do and experience, the larger their vocabulary will be. A low socio-economic background limits the opportunities for variety of experience. Reading is one avenue for new experience and thus for vocabulary learning and enrichment. It is thus useful to see vocabulary size as a symptom, and so the main focus should be on providing a variety of engaging and meaningful experiences with language and supporting vocabulary knowledge through this experience. Focusing on vocabulary growth alone is missing the point.

Just as reading can be a source of experience and vocabulary growth, movies, TV and the internet can also be a source of experience and vocabulary growth. Hobbies and interests outside school also support vocabulary growth. Schmitt (2019) reviews the evidence that learners of English as a second language learn a great deal of English through various multimedia sources. Although parents may be concerned that their children are over-exposed to multimedia, it nevertheless is a fruitful source of vocabulary knowledge.

Suggestions for improving vocabulary learning through quantity of reading and writing

1. There should be an increase in the amount of reading and writing done in class time in most subjects. The principle which lies behind this suggestion is the time-on-task principle which says that the more you do something, the better you will become at doing it. This is a rather crude principle because it ignores the quality of work that is being done and focuses on quantity. However, it is a very effective principle. A major factor in becoming a good reader is to do lots of reading. A major factor in becoming a good writer is to do lots of writing. Its strength is that it is a fairly straightforward principle to apply, and it provides for plenty of opportunities for learning.

   As a reading goal, learners should read at least 500,000 running words per school year. This is actually a modest reading goal. It works out to be around 2,500 words per school subject per week. In social sciences, this equals about seven pages of a social science text.

   As a writing goal, learners should write at least 40,000 running words per school year. This works out to be 1000 words per school week, or 200 words per school subject per week.

   Before implementing this principle. it would be useful to work out how much reading and writing learners are doing at present to get some kind of baseline measure. Our suspicion with very little evidence is that teachers avoid giving learners reading and writing tasks because they fear they will be unable and unwilling to do them.
2. There should be a one-on-one diagnostic program to identify and support those who need help. This may not be a very large group of students, but some help could make a great difference to their reading and to their general progress in school.

3. Eventually, the amount of in-school reading and writing should be at least partly matched by that done outside of class time.

Suggestions for giving attention to vocabulary

Although vocabulary needs to be closely related to its use, some deliberate partly-decontextualized attention will have a strong effect on learning (Elley, 1989). This is especially true if this attention involves multiple encounters involving retrieval, varied meetings and use, and analysis and enrichment.

1. The vocabulary which is most likely to be unfamiliar to native-speakers at secondary school is the topic-related vocabulary of the various subject areas. Learners should see and hear this vocabulary with the words written on the board if there is not a written text accompanying the lesson.
2. When a topic word occurs, it should be briefly explained and where possible analyzed for its parts and its relationship to already known words. If it occurs in a set phrase, the phrase should also be given attention and analyzed.
3. Regular attention should be given to word consciousness. Chapter 9 of *What every Primary School Teacher should Know about Vocabulary* (van Hees & Nation, 2017) deals with this. Of particular importance is giving attention to word parts (affixes and stems), dictionary use (including various kinds of electronic look-up), and the core meaning of words.
4. Learners should receive regular training in how to learn. This should involve particular attention to vocabulary but should emphasize that the principles of learning apply much more widely than just vocabulary. The learning principles covered in this training should include, in order of importance, spaced repetition, retrieval (recall), balancing opportunities for learning (the four strands), deliberate attention and analysis and elaboration, varied meetings and varied use, and time on task. See van Hees & Nation, Chapter 5 (2017) and Webb & Nation, Chapters 4 and 5 (2017) for more on these principles.
5. Teaching opposites and members of a lexical set together may make learning more difficult (Nation, 2000). Dealing with vocabulary as it occurs in texts avoids interference problems.

How can reading be encouraged and monitored in class?

1. Use at least one quarter of the class time for the learners to do focused reading.
2. Encourage and monitor the reading by using the activities in the texts, and by developing quick quizzes and information transfer tasks.

3. Make reading an enjoyable interactive activity for some of the reading. Get the learners to work in pairs during the reading, to quickly report back to the class on the reading, and to make questions for others to answer.
4. Use engaging questioning techniques, such as, guess the questions, see the questions before reading, and adding a competitive element if desirable.
5. In some part of the school program, learners should do a speed reading course. This takes about 10 minutes a day, three days a week, for about seven or eight weeks. Sonia Millett's material at <https://www.wgtn.ac.nz/lals/resources> contains free speed reading courses. These were written for learners of English as a foreign language, but the highest level course could be used by native-speakers.
6. Find ways of rewarding learners for the quantity of reading that they do.
7. Keep a record of the amount of reading done each week in terms of words read.
8. Make sure that when reading is the goal, a lot of time is not taken away from reading by the activities related to reading.
9. Have extra reading available for faster readers.

The goal is to increase the amount of reading that learners do, while decreasing the work the teacher has to do. Teachers should teach less and rely on reading more.

How can writing be encouraged and monitored in class?

1. Initially train and encourage copying. Train learners in the skill of delayed copying (Hill, 1969). In delayed copying, learners look at the text, hold in their head as much of meaningful part of a sentence that they can, look away and then write that part down without looking back. This continues until all the text is copied.
2. Initially respond to ideas not form. Pointing out errors too early on can discourage production.
3. Provide opportunities for a variety of forms of writing – answering questions, filling tables, taking notes, writing a short report, and writing an essay or assignment. Make sure that there is at least one extended (at least a page) piece of writing each week.
4. Find ways of rewarding learners for the quantity of writing that they do.
5. Teachers should develop an understanding of the parts of writing process and use this in observing and analysing written work (goals of the writer, gathering ideas, organising ideas, ideas to text, reviewing, editing, model of the reader) (Nation & Macalister, 2021, Chapter 8).
6. Find a way for each learner to keep their pieces of writing together, so that they can be used for measuring progress, for keeping a record of the quantity

written, and for gaining useful feedback. Building up a portfolio of writing has many positive effects for motivation, diagnosis and assessment.
7. Encourage use of typing tutor and voice recognition programs to increase writing speed.
8. Be careful that the demands of writing do not limit the amount of reading that learners are doing.
9. Find ways of giving learners plenty to write about – read and recall, listen and recall, write from experience, write from several sources.
10. Writing provides an opportunity for multiple encounters with the same ideas and vocabulary. Consider this when setting topics to write about.

Teen-agers learn on average around three words per day (around 1000 words a year). This amount of learning can be increased by increasing the variety of receptive and productive language experience, and by giving some persistent regular deliberate attention to vocabulary.

Suggestions for learning through multimedia resources

Young native-speakers of English do not need encouragement to play video games and multi-player online games (MMOGs), search the web, watch movies and TV shows, and listen to and sing pop songs. There is plenty of evidence from learning English as a foreign language that contextual vocabulary learning (Elgort et al., 2018) occurs from multimedia resources (de Wilde, Brysbaert, & Eyckmans, 2019; Schmitt, 2019). The conditions supporting vocabulary learning are the same for multimedia resources as they are for other sources of vocabulary learning. Repetition through quantity of language input and good quality meetings and uses of vocabulary are needed for learning to occur. The following criteria provide a way of at least initially evaluating the learning opportunities for vocabulary learning.

1. Are the children interested and engaged in the activity.
2. Is the activity language rich and does it involve some unfamiliar vocabulary?
3. Does the activity have opportunities for repeated attention to the same vocabulary?
4. Do the repeated opportunities involve varied contexts and varied uses of the vocabulary?
5. Do the children have opportunities to produce the vocabulary?
6. Does the activity involve language interaction with others?

Let us apply the criteria to some multimedia activities. Performing karaoke, for example, is a language rich activity. Pop songs use largely high-frequency vocabulary

(Tegge, 2017) and so for native-speakers, the vocabulary learning potential may be rather limited. The nature of pop songs and rehearsal can provide plenty of repetition. There is little in the way of varied contexts, but there is certainly the opportunity to produce the vocabulary. Being able to see the words as well as hear them is of great benefit to vocabulary learning and increases the chances that the words will be processed for their meaning rather than just their sung form.

Watching movies is an interesting and engaging activity. Analysis of the vocabulary in movies shows that movies include a typical range of high-frequency, mid-frequency and low-frequency vocabulary (Webb, 2010; Webb & Rodgers, 2009a & b), and so are likely to contain some unfamiliar vocabulary. The topic vocabulary of the movie is likely to contain some unknown words and because of their topic-relatedness are likely to be repeated in varied contexts. If the movie contains captions this could help the noticing and learning of unfamiliar vocabulary. Typically movies do not involve language production and interaction with others. Young children may watch a favourite movie over and over and may memorize and act out the movie with others in play.

Multimedia resources provide variety of language input, and variety of language input, particularly with a variety of topics, provides opportunities to meet a wider variety of vocabulary (Sutarsyah, Nation, & Kennedy, 1994). Multimedia resources increase the richness of vocabulary learning and need to be seen positively. Watching TV, playing games, and interacting through the internet are not mindless activities and support vocabulary growth.

Supporting vocabulary growth in adults

One of the native-speakers who was interviewed as part of the Coxhead, Nation & Sim (2014) study on versions of the Vocabulary Size Test reported that taking the test, "… feels like things get triggered way down deep in your memory. Deep in your memory gland. It's like looking for something in the bottom of your handbag." In other words, some of the words in the test were known, but they were not easily accessed in her memory. This image of a 'memory gland' is striking, as is the image of the handbag. In this section, we look at ways to increase vocabulary size and keep vocabulary active in our 'memory glands'.

Appendix 2 contains the feedback sheet used in the adult vocabulary size testing research reported in Coxhead, Nation, & Sim, 2014) and adapted for the secondary school project (Coxhead, Nation, & Sim, 2015) for test takers whose vocabulary test results showed they had vocabulary sizes of 10,000 word families or more. There were feedback sheets in both studies for vocabulary sizes of 1,000–5,000 words and 6,000–10,000 words. The basic principles of the feedback are that people who want to increase their vocabulary size should read more and should read every day, thereby increasing their input. The reading should also be wide ranging, so that there is a variety of kinds of input in reading (e.g. magazines, newspapers, novels) but also in listening (such as radio and tv programs and podcasts on non-fiction topics of high interest). One of the highest scoring students in the secondary school study (Coxhead, Nation, & Sim, 2015) reported that he was reading quantum physics in his spare time (at age 13) and this was confirmed by his teacher. It is important to spend time talking about the content and ideas from those programs whenever possible. Talking about the content provides opportunities to recall words that have occurred in the input and to use them in speaking.

Another set of suggestions focused on using strategies such as word cards and notebooks to help with deliberate learning of words, paying attention to words in texts and their spelling as well as meaning, and the words they commonly occur with. Seeking opportunities to use newly acquired words in speaking or writing is another strategy for increasing vocabulary size. Using words is important for building memory and for making words part of our active vocabulary. Our colleague and friend, Professor Graeme Kennedy, used to tell a story about using the word *cogent* for the first time when he was at university and being very aware that he knew the word well but had never previously used it productively. There is a certain amount of risk with using words productively if there is uncertainty about meaning or use, but it is an opportunity to get feedback on use from those around us.

Noticing words and paying attention to them or making a note of them is a very useful way of picking up new words. It is important to ensure that any meeting with these new words happens quickly after the first meeting, so that there is less opportunity for forgetting. For people learning English as a foreign language, we often suggest to learners that they become vocabulary detectives, and investigate new words that are useful to them by looking them up in dictionaries, keeping track of them, noting the words that commonly occur with them, and try to use them. These same ideas can apply to native-speakers who want to increase their vocabulary size in English. Finally, Coxhead & Bytheway (2015) report on vocabulary growth through playing Massive Online Multi-player Role Playing Games (MMORPG) such as World of Warcraft. During piloting for the 20,000 versions of the Vocabulary Size Test, it was clear that a group of young Malaysian men who took the tests had much higher scores than their counterparts. When asked what their secret to a large vocabulary size was, they said that they all played MMORPGs. Coxhead & Bytheway (2015) attribute this increase in vocabulary knowledge to factors such as large amounts of time on task, opportunities for interaction and language use, large amounts of input, and huge motivation to play. Learners also learn through observing others playing. As one of the learners who is a regular MMORPG player noted, these games are so absorbing, that he didn't even blink at times when he was playing.

The advice in this chapter looking at supporting native-speaker vocabulary growth involves several common themes that apply at all age levels.

1. Interact with others in topic-related talk that thoughtfully explores challenging ideas.
2. Do lots of sustained reading on a variety of topics.
3. Get involved in thoughtful listening and multimedia activities involving plenty of language use.
4. Take up opportunities to write as a way of revisiting ideas and discovering new ideas.
5. Develop word consciousness involving a variety of deliberate focuses on vocabulary.
6. Understand the basic principles of learning including the importance of spaced repetition, retrieval, varied meetings and varied use, elaboration through analysis and association, deliberate attention, using a balance of different kinds of learning opportunities, and taking control of your own learning.

Vocabulary learning occurs because the basic conditions of repetition and quality of processing are met. The above suggestions are ways of encouraging these conditions to occur.

In the next chapter we look at ways of measuring vocabulary learning.

CHAPTER 9

Measures and item types used to estimate native-speaker vocabulary size

Measuring vocabulary size involves finding out how many words someone knows. In this chapter we look at how "knowing" is measured. Descriptions of what is involved in knowing a word cover many aspects of word knowledge (Nation, 2013, Chapter 2). Knowing a word involves knowing its form, meaning and use and each of these three broad aspects includes receptive and productive knowledge. Knowing a word's form involves being able to recognize and produce its spoken form and its written form. It also involves knowing its morphology (its word parts). Knowing a word's meaning involves being able to connect a word's form and its meaning, knowing a concept for the word and having a range of associations with the word. Knowing a word's use involves being familiar with its part of speech, its grammar, its collocations and any restrictions on its use. No test can measure all of these aspects of knowledge, and so measures of vocabulary size focus on being able to recognise or produce the form of a word and being able to relate that form to a known meaning. Vocabulary size tests typically do not indicate how well a learner can use a word either receptively of productively, and how rich their knowledge of the word is. As we shall see, this has led to dissatisfaction with some item types, and raises the question of *How well do you have to know a word before we can say that you really know it?* Some researchers are satisfied with giving credit for partial knowledge of some words, while others want much stronger knowledge of each word.

Throughout this book we have looked at a range of factors that affect the measurement of native-speaker vocabulary size. One of those factors is the measure or test item that we use to measure vocabulary size. Each kind of measure or test item draws on certain kinds of knowledge about a word and certain minimum strengths of knowledge. Each kind of measure or item type has its own strengths and weaknesses. In this chapter we look critically at a range of commonly used measures and item types. We will find that for largely practical reasons, the measures and item types used relate closely to the age and development of the native-speakers who are being tested.

Using spoken output to measure vocabulary size and growth

Single person output studies

In Chapter 2 we looked at using children's spoken output as a way of measuring vocabulary size and vocabulary growth. The studies done in the early 1900s tried to find total vocabulary size by counting every word a young child produced. If only relatively small samples of a child's speech are taken, this approach is unlikely to provide a valid measure of vocabulary size because the children will not have had enough opportunity to produce what they know. At best, such studies can provide accounts of minimum vocabulary knowledge, but this in itself is interesting because there is a tendency for teachers especially to underestimate how many words their learners know. When output studies show young children knowing hundreds and possibly thousands of words, teachers need to be aware that their native-speaker learners already have substantial vocabulary knowledge when they start their schooling.

The studies done in the early 1900s were restricted by the need for a researcher to be present to write down what was spoken. Modern technology makes the job much easier, but some of the same methodological issues still apply. Foremost amongst these is the unit of counting, namely, what is counted as a different word. There needs to be transparency and consistency in deciding the size of the unit to be counted (type, lemma, flemma, level of word family), as well as an explicit justification for the choice of the particular unit. Nation (2016, Section 2) looks at a range of items that need to be considered when deciding what to count as words and what to count as the same word.

There is still much to be learned from studies that try to measure a very young native-speaker's vocabulary size and growth by recording and analysing their spoken output. Such studies would need to involve substantial amounts of output because Zipf's Law is likely to apply, where half of the different words will occur only once.

Studies using small amounts of output

Output studies which use small amounts of output as indicators of vocabulary growth are not truly measuring vocabulary growth because there are so many different factors besides vocabulary knowledge that affect the number of different words produced (see Chapter 2). In addition, several of these factors are likely to have a stronger effect than vocabulary knowledge on the number of different words produced.

There are several ways of dealing with this problem. One way is to carry on using the number of types produced but to explain that this is not a measure of vocabulary size or growth but is a measure that predicts later vocabulary size. This preserves the status quo but better describes what is being measured.

Another solution is to try to control the variables of the number of tokens, the variety of topics, the quality of parental support during the interaction, the intrusiveness of the data-gathering, and the unit of counting. Several studies have worked on controlling these variables with a reasonable degree of success. Controlling these variables will still be unlikely to provide an uncontaminated measure of vocabulary growth, but it will be better than current practice.

Another option is to use an as-yet-untried measure of vocabulary richness in this kind of research – vocabulary profiling. Vocabulary profiling involves using a computer program such as AntWordProfiler to run the child's output through word frequency lists, or better still through lists based on Biemiller's (2010) *Words Worth Teaching* which sequences words according to the likelihood of them being known. If sequenced lists of perhaps 100 words each were used, a child's vocabulary output could be rated on vocabulary richness according to the levels that the words used came from. A young child who used some words from the 700 word level or above for example would get a higher rating than a child who did not use any or many words beyond that level.

Yet another option is to use a receptive measure of vocabulary size such as the Picture Vocabulary Size Test or some version of it with very young children. Lonigan and Milburn (2017) present evidence that at least for very young children receptive and productive (expressive) vocabulary represent a single vocabulary knowledge factor. With a small vocabulary, there is little point in distinguishing receptive and productive vocabulary knowledge because a child is likely to be able to produce almost all of the words they know in one form or other. However, it is difficult however to get young children to take a test seriously as there are so many distractions even within the test itself.

Because of the difficulty of using standardised receptive measures with very young children (18 months to three-years-old), some researchers use an indirect measure where parents indicate what words their children know (Fernald, Marchman, & Weisleder, 2013; Mancilla-Martinez, Pan, & Vagh, 2011). In this kind of measure, a parent checks on a list of words (typically the 680 item list of the MacArthur-Bates Communicative Developmental Inventory: Words and Sentences) the words that their child "understands and says". For children under-three-years old, this is arguably a measure of total vocabulary size, particularly if the list contains most of the words that children are likely to know at that age. The weakness of the measure is that it is not directly based on what the child does but is based on a parent's recall (see Heilman, Weismer, Evans, & Hollar, 2005 for an evaluation).

Measuring receptive vocabulary size

The most popular test item formats for measuring receptive vocabulary size are the Yes/No format with pseudo-words included as a check against guessing (Brysbaert et al., 2015), the multiple-choice format consisting of a stem (a single word or a word in a non-defining context) and four meaning choices (Coxhead, Nation, & Sim, 2015), and the interview format with the word in a context and the test-takers required to provide some indication through explanation or gesture of the word's meaning (Biemiller, 2005). The Picture Vocabulary Size Test uses a multiple-choice format with four picture choices.

Each format has its own strengths and weaknesses but in studies involving learners of English as a foreign language, there has been debate over whether various formats provide a demanding enough measure to be able to say that a learner getting an item correct knows each word well enough to make use of it in reading or listening (Kremmel & Schmitt, 2016).

What do scores on different vocabulary test item formats mean?

Several studies have looked at the relationship between different vocabulary test item formats, showing that different formats give different results (Paul, Stallman, & O'Rourke, 1990; Waring & Takaki, 2003; Laufer, Elder, Hill, & Congdon, 2004; Kremmel & Schmitt, 2016). Different test item formats are likely to measure different strengths of vocabulary knowledge and different kinds of vocabulary knowledge. While this can be seen as a problem, it can also be seen as a very useful feature of test items because it allows researchers to examine a variety of aspects of knowing a word, and to see the cumulative growth of knowledge of a word. The Waring and Takaki (2003) study involving learners of English as a foreign language on vocabulary learning from reading, for example, used three different test formats testing the same words and showed that as a result of reading a text containing unknown words (pseudo-words) learners gained receptive written form recognition knowledge of 15.3 of the 25 tested words, receptive written recognition knowledge of the meaning of 10.6 of the 25 words, and receptive written recall knowledge of the meaning of 4.6 of the 25 words on the immediate post-test. That is, the learners showed a variety of strengths of kinds of knowledge of the target words with a small number being learned quite well, a larger number known not quite so well and a much larger number just beginning to be known.

Tests of low or moderate difficulty place a ceiling on the strength of knowledge that can be shown, and tests of high difficulty similarly impose a floor effect on showing what is known. Let us clarify this with some examples.

If a learner gets a receptive multiple-choice item correct, such as an item in the Vocabulary Size Test, because of the ceiling effect of the item, we do not know if the learner could also get a more difficult test item on the same word correct, such as a receptive meaning-recall test where they have to provide a synonym or explanation for the word. On the other hand, the multiple-choice format allows the learner to draw on partial knowledge of the word meaning that might not be demonstrated in their response to the more difficult recall test. As Nagy, Herman, and Anderson (1985) have shown, different kinds of receptive multiple-choice items allow the learners to draw on different ranges of strength of knowledge.

If we made a scale from weak knowledge to strong knowledge, then we could use it to try to show the ranges of knowledge that learners could draw on for various test item formats. Meaning-recall items such as interviews and translation tests require at least reasonably strong knowledge of the meaning. To correctly answer the item, the learner can only draw on a narrow range of strength of knowledge, and that strength of knowledge is at the demanding end of the scale. To correctly answer a Yes/No item however, the learner can draw on a very wide range of knowledge ranging from partial knowledge of the word form to very strong knowledge of the word. To correctly answer a multiple-choice item, a learner needs at least more knowledge than the minimum knowledge required for Yes/No.

```
Weak ______________________________________________________________Strong
          <- Yes/No ------------------------------------------------------>
                    <- Multiple-choice ---------------------------------->
                                                   <- Meaning-recall --->
```

A problem with items like Yes/No and multiple-choice is that for any particular word we do not know what strength of knowledge is being drawn on. Kremmel and Schmitt (2016) for example show that 56.7% of the words correct on their multiple-choice measure were also correct on their meaning recall measure. For some of the other words which were correct on the multiple-choice measure, the meaning-recall measure was just too difficult for them, even though they knew enough to get the multiple-choice measure correct.

When choosing which item format to use, it is useful to consider what degree of knowledge you are prepared to give credit for, that is, where you are willing for the weak end of your knowledge scale to be. If you are testing with the purpose of seeing what learning and teaching needs to be done or for diagnostic purposes, then a multiple-choice test may be a very suitable format, because even partial knowledge of a word is useful. If the testing is to see if learners are likely to be able to read well, then a more demanding item format would be appropriate.

A danger with using a difficult item format is to assume that getting the item wrong indicates a complete lack of knowledge. An answer may be wrong because of a complete lack of knowledge, but it may also be wrong because the item format did not allow the learner to draw on existing partial knowledge.

Issues with multiple-choice measures

Multiple-choice answers must be carefully made, making sure that the correct answer is not signalled by the length of the choice or some other distinguishing feature. Dale and O'Rourke (1981), for example, who made thousands of vocabulary test items, set out criteria for making items which include positioning the correct answer by random choice, making sure choices are roughly the same length, controlling the difficulty of the language in the choices, and not using distractors based on spelling discrimination. In vocabulary tests, it is also important to make sure that the distractors relate to words at the same frequency level or knowledge level as the word being tested.

Multiple-choice measures are difficult to make but they are easy to administer and score. Because they provide choices, they can be answered using partial knowledge, but they also make guessing possible (Stewart, 2014). One way to control for guessing is to include an *I don't know* option. Research with foreign language learners (Zhang, 2013; McDonald & Asaba, 2015; Stoeckel, Bennett, & McLean, 2016; Stoeckel, Stewart, McLean, Ishii, Kramer, & Matsumoto, 2019) suggests that, because different learners vary in their use of this option (some use it and some never use it), it is better not to include it as an option. The use of an *I don't know* option may also lead to moving through the test more quickly because of less careful consideration of the choices (Zhang, 2013).

The strongest criticism of multiple-choice for measuring vocabulary size is that the construct of meaning-recognition does not relate well to normal language use, whereas the construct of meaning-recall, where the learner sees a word and has to recall a meaning, is more like what happens when we read or listen (Gyllstad, Vilkaite, & Schmitt, 2015; Kremmel & Schmitt, 2016; Stewart, 2014).

Stoeckel, Stewart, McLean, Ishii, Kramer, & Matsumoto (2019) approached the issue of item format in a very practical way. While a meaning-recall format would be likely to provide a more valid measure of vocabulary size, if there is a predictable relationship between meaning-recognition and meaning-recall, then the more practical meaning-recognition format could be used with an appropriate downwards score adjustment to estimate reading vocabulary size. They found a strong correlation (0.9) between the Vocabulary Size Test and a meaning-recall test of the same words. For learners of English as a foreign language, the meaning-recognition Vocabulary Size Test gave much higher scores, and we would expect the same for native-speakers of English. Although the meaning-recognition Vocabulary Size Test could be used as a proxy for the meaning-recall version, research is needed to determine the size and nature of a score adjustment. However, meaning-recognition (multiple-choice) may be a useful enough measure for tracking the vocabulary growth of native-speakers of English across different age levels to keep using it without adjustment, as long as it is borne in mind that the scores may be inflated because of guessing. Stoeckel et al. (2019) suggest using shortened versions of the Vocabulary Size Test so that test-takers do not have to sit tests containing lots of items way beyond their current level of knowledge. This possibility becomes much more feasible with the availability of prevalence norms showing the likelihood that a word will be known such as those generously made available by Brysbaert, Mandera, McCormick, & Keuleers (2019). Dale and O'Rourke's (1981) *Living Word Vocabulary* and Biemiller's (2010) *Words Worth Teaching* provide similar prevalence data for younger native-speakers.

Issues with Yes/No measures

Yes/No measures involve test-takers seeing a word and making a Yes/No decision about whether they could provide a meaning for that word. They do not have to provide the meaning. The accuracy of the test is checked by including a large number of pseudo-words in the test. In the Brysbaert et al. (2016) study, these made up around one-third of the test items. The pseudo-words look like possible English words because they follow regular English spelling rules. A test-taker's score on the test is reduced by the number of pseudo-words that the test-taker said they knew (false alarms), and researchers have tried a wide variety of means to adjust scores (Huibregtse, Admiraal, & Meara, 2002; Pellicer-Sanchez & Schmitt, 2012; Stubbe, 2012; Stubbe & Stewart, 2012), including no adjustment (Mochida & Harrington, 2006).

It is important that there are very clear instructions about how test-takers should decide if they will respond with Yes or No. They should not make the decision simply on familiarity with the form of the word. On the other hand, they should not feel obliged to say No if they know the word but would struggle to define it.

One problem with Yes/No tests is face validity. Test-takers have to indicate whether they could give a meaning for a word, but they don't actually have to give a meaning. The validity of the test then depends on the honesty of the test-takers. As we saw in Chapter 6, Diack (1975b) asked test-takers to check themselves by looking up the last words they said they knew in a dictionary. This was not a check on honesty but rather accuracy. Test-takers may sincerely think they know a word (or a non-word), but they may be mis-led by partial formal similarity or some other cause. This makes the creation of pseudo-words for the test a matter of some importance. Early versions of the Yes/No test used pseudo-words made by making small changes to real words, but this method ran the risk of the pseudo-word being too close to a real word so that test-takers may have sincerely thought they were known. Brysbaert et al. (2016) used an algorithm called Wuggy (Keuleers & Brysbaert, 2010) to create their pseudo-words which followed the spelling rules of English. For a review of Wuggy, an evaluation of pseudowords and an automatic method of creating them in English and other languages, see König, Calude, & Coxhead (2019).

Yes/No tests also allow test-takers to draw on a wide range of strengths of word knowledge to respond to a word, and they could thus come under similar criticisms as multiple-choice tests in giving credit for partial knowledge which is not strong enough to allow coping with the word in reading or listening.

The strength of the Yes/No measure is its simplicity. Yes/No tests are very easy to make, fast and easy to administer, well suited to computerization, and easy to score. An adult native-speaker sitting a Yes/No test typically feels satisfied with the experience and takes such a test seriously. Several studies show strong correlations between Yes/No tests and multiple-choice, translation, or interview tests (Eyckmans, 2004; Mochida & Harrington, 2006; Stubbe, 2012; Lemhöfer & Broersma, 2012).

Yes/No tests are typically tests of isolated words. There are good reasons for including a non-defining context sentence for each tested word. Here are some examples taken from the Vocabulary Size Test. Notice that the context is written in very well-known English words and does not give away the meaning. The tested word is in italics.

Can they *maintain* it?
He sat on a *stone*.
I am *upset*.
The *drawer* was empty.

Putting the tested word in a context sentence would allow the testing of homonyms and homographs such as *ball* (a round object, a social event) and *bank* (a landform, a financial business) (Parent, 2012). Homonyms and homographs account for around 10% of English vocabulary and so it would be good not to exclude them from vocabulary size tests (Goulden, Nation, & Read, 1990). Using a sentence context orients the test-taker to the part of speech of the word and provides a favorable opportunity for retrieving the word. In this respect the test is a little more like language use. When test-takers look at lists of isolated words, a feeling of unreality starts to set in because the words are seen more as forms than as living words. A context sentence helps avoid this. The disadvantages of context sentences are that they have to be made and checked, and they increase the amount of time taken to sit the test. The advantages however far outweigh the disadvantages.

Issues with meaning-recall (interview) measures

The role of multiple-choice items in vocabulary size tests has been the focus of welcome scrutiny (Stewart, 2014; Gyllstad, Vilkaite, & Schmitt, 2015). One of the major criticisms of the use of the multiple-choice format in the Vocabulary Size Test is that it is not clear whether this format measures the kind of vocabulary knowledge needed for reading, or more broadly, it is not clear what type of knowledge and what depth of knowledge the multiple-choice format is measuring in vocabulary size tests. A suggested alternative to multiple-choice is an interview test where learners need to recall the meaning of each given word form. It is argued that such a meaning-recall test (Schmitt, 2010: 86) is a better approximation of the kind of knowledge needed for real world activities like listening and reading than meaning-recognition is. Gyllstad, Vilkaite, & Schmitt (2015) compared meaning-recall with meaning-recognition for the 3,000, 6,000 and 9,000 bands of the Vocabulary Size Test. For the 3,000 and 6,000 bands, 80% of the words were answered in the same way (known or unknown) on both tests. For the 9,000 band, there was 70% agreement. Between 11% (for the 6,000 band) and 26% (for the 9,000 band) of the words were correct in the meaning-recognition test but not in the meaning-recall test. Gyllstad, Vilkaite, and Schmitt looked closely into some learners answering words at the 3,000 level. They found little evidence of blind guessing (around 4% of answers), but they found evidence of test-taking strategies. Some of the difference between the two tests was vocabulary-knowledge based and comes from the different sensitivity of the tests to partial knowledge. Some comes from the differences in the format of the tests and relates to the nature of the task. Each test format brings its own confounding factors. The Gyllstad, Vilkaite, and Schmitt study involved learners of English as a foreign language. Such learners are particularly suited to comparing meaning-recognition and meaning recall formats because first language translations can be used as a means of meaning-recall. One of the issues with meaning-recall with native-speakers of a language is the difficulty native-speakers may have in explaining the meanings of words. This is accompanied by the difficulty in scoring the explanation.

The receptive multiple-choice format and the receptive interview format (meaning-recall) are both measures of receptive knowledge in that they provide the word form and ask the learner to demonstrate knowledge of the meaning of the word. We know that meaning-recognition measures are easier than meaning-recall measures (Laufer, Elder, Hill, & Congdon, 2004; Laufer & Goldstein, 2004), so a meaning-recall measure requires stronger knowledge than a multiple-choice measure. However, answering a multiple-choice item can be done on the basis of strong knowledge or weak knowledge. This can be seen as a strength or weakness of the multiple-choice item format depending on the purposes of the test. A meaning-recall test requires the ability and the strength of knowledge to articulate a meaning or some approximation of the meaning (Biemiller & Slonim, 2001). The multiple-choice format allows a correct answer to be made on the basis of any strength of knowledge on a much wider scale. That is, a multiple-choice item can give the learner credit for a degree of partial knowledge that would not allow the learner to answer an interview test. This is a disadvantage of the multiple-choice format, if the test-maker wants to have a relatively clear idea of what standard of knowledge is being measured by the test. It is an advantage however if the test-maker wants to give credit for as much as possible of the previous learning that has occurred. A meaning-recall test will underestimate the previous learning that has occurred for some items in the test. A meaning-recognition test will give credit for some knowledge that may not yet be strong enough for normal language use. The amount of this under-estimation and over-estimation will depend largely on the relationship between the learner's vocabulary size and the particular frequency levels being tested. That is, it seems more likely that most under-estimation and over-estimation will occur at the upper boundaries of a learner's vocabulary knowledge.

How big is the difference between meaning recognition and meaning recall? Laufer and Goldstein (2004) testing learners of English as a foreign language found a big difference between meaning-recognition (passive recognition) and meaning-recall (passive recall), for example, with meaning-recall scores (13.07/30) on the Academic Word List level being half the size of the meaning recognition scores (26.79/30). Laufer and Goldstein's meaning-recall format provided the word form followed by the first letter of its first language translation. This is a less forgiving format than one where learners can be given credit for any one of a variety of answers. Gyllstad, Vilkaite, and Schmitt (2015) allowed first language or second language answers, a defining example or an illustration. Test-takers were however required to give some detail in their answer (*celery* = 'a vegetable' was not sufficient, but *celery* = 'a vegetable' plus some additional description such as 'long and green' was adequate). The difference between their meaning-recognition and meaning-recall scores was not so great, at between 11% to 26% higher scores for meaning-recognition. Table 9.1 compares features of meaning-recall and meaning-recognition tests.

In Table 9.1 the multiple-choice format is said to provide opportunity for recall and recognition. Where a tested word is well-known, recall could be used to quickly choose the correct answer. Where a tested word is not well-known, there may be little or any recall before carefully examining the choices.

Table 9.1 Features of two receptive vocabulary measures

Feature	Multiple-choice	Interview
Aspects of word knowledge tested	Word-form recognition Word-meaning recognition Form-meaning connection	Word-form recognition Word-meaning recall Form-meaning connection
Strength of knowledge	Recognition or recall	Recall
Compensatory procedures: vocabulary knowledge	If using a meaning-recognition test for measuring what vocabulary has been learned, expect the vocabulary size score to be about right except for low frequency cognates and loan words.	If using a meaning-recall test for measuring what vocabulary has been learned, expect the vocabulary size score to be a considerable underestimate.
Compensatory procedures: language use	If using a meaning-recognition test for measuring the vocabulary required for reading, expect the vocabulary size score to be larger than the vocabulary level of the optimal reading material.	If using a meaning-recall test for measuring the vocabulary required for reading, expect the vocabulary size score to be about the same or a little lower than the vocabulary level of the optimal reading material.

What kind of knowledge should a test of vocabulary size measure?

The type of item used in a vocabulary size test will depend on the age of the test-takers and the kind of knowledge seen as being appropriate for the purposes of the test. For all test-takers, the results from a test will be affected by the attitude of those taking the test, and the administration of the test needs to take this into account, often by administering the test one-on-one with appropriate support to keep the test-taker on task.

Young children

Young children beginning to speak or in the early stages of learning to speak do not respond well to formal testing, and it is much more convenient to use counts of the different words produced by children as a measure of their vocabulary size and growth. We have looked at the issues involved in this kind of measure in Chapter 2.

For children as young as 18 months and 24 months, Fernald, Marchman, and Weisleder (2013) used two item multiple-choice with pictures (Looking-while-Listening). The children's reactions were video-recorded and the videos were analysed by raters to determine what picture children were looking at after they heard the cue sentences. A high level of agreement was reached in the ratings. A weakness of some studies using this Looking-while-Listening measure was to use more words in the test with children when they were older than in the test that was used when they were younger. This makes comparison between the age levels uncertain because the older children can gain higher scores because they have more items to answer. Nonetheless, the use of two-choice picture items seems to work with young children.

Some measures of vocabulary knowledge use a multiple-choice format with pictures as the choices. Among the best known of these is the Peabody Picture Vocabulary Test (PPVT) (Dunn, 1965). In this test, learners hear a word and then point to one of four pictures to indicate the meaning of the word. Testing stops after six consecutive errors. Because the words in the test are not a representative sample drawn from a larger population of words, the Peabody Picture Vocabulary Test is not a measure of total vocabulary size. It is however a very useful measure for comparing children. Most of the 204 words tested in the PPVT are from the first to tenth 1000 according to the BNC/COCA lists. The words are unlikely to have been chosen randomly to represent those levels, as the only substantial list available at the time the test was made in the early 1960s was the Thorndike and Lorge (1944) list. All the words are nouns, verbs or adjectives. There are five very low frequency words beyond the 20th 1000 that most people are unlikely to know. These seem to have been included to ensure no-one gets every item correct on the test.

Primary school children

Biemiller and Slonim (2001) directly tested a representative sample of words, by using an interview test. They put each word in a context to partly guide the children, and asked them to describe the meaning of the test word. Using the same sample as in their words in context test, Biemiller and Boote (2006) compared a multiple-choice picture test with their sentence-context test finding higher scores in the picture test. Biemiller (2005, p. 229) considered that while the sentence-context test tended to underestimate vocabulary size, largely because of the difficulties young children have in explaining what a word means, a multiple-choice test may over-estimate children's *effective* vocabulary.

The Picture Vocabulary Size Test has been looked at in Chapter 4. It was designed for young-native-speakers who could not yet read, although a written sentence is presented along with each spoken sentence in the test. Once children can read, then the Vocabulary Size Test in a reduced form is a suitable test for primary school children. As we have seen, the multiple-choice format gives credit for partial knowledge and scores may be inflated by the use of test-taking strategies.

Secondary school children

No questions in two versions of the Vocabulary Size Test were answered correctly by every one of 247 native-speakers sitting the VST. For each question there was at least one native-speaker who got it wrong, Every teen-age native-speaker is certain to know all of the very high frequency words from at least the first 3000 words, but they make mistakes in answering items from these levels in the test. Why?

When considering the accuracy of a vocabulary size test, it is worth considering the range of factors that may be involved in measuring vocabulary size.

1. Unfamiliarity with the format of the test: One native-speaker sitting the computerised VST did not answer the first block of five questions because they mistakenly pushed the continue button which took them to the next block. Because each question represents 200 words, this meant 1000 words less on their vocabulary size measure. The good administration of a test involves practice with trial items and the opportunity to ask questions so that the test procedures are clear.
2. Failure to apply a sensible test-taking strategy: The VST and the PVST are multiple-choice tests and when sitting such tests, test-takers need to apply a sensible strategy by taking their time, considering all choices before making an answer, and eliminating obviously incorrect answers. Some test-takers may wish to rush through a test, and may be encouraged in this by the high familiarity of the early items in the test. Rushing through may be even more likely in the later stages of the test involving the very low frequency items where very few words are likely to be known. Even among the low frequency items in a vocabulary size test, there are words which are likely to be known for a variety of reasons (*seesaw, celebrant, quoit, layabout, pterodactyl*) and these words may be skipped over because they occur amongst a sea of unfamiliar words. Monitored individual administration of the test can reduce these problems especially if the administrator uses the monitoring to train the test-taker in useful strategies.
3. Willingness to guess: A multiple-choice test allows the possibility of correctly guessing an answer. Learners differ in their willingness to guess (McDonald & Asaba, 2015). Adding an *I don't know* option does not solve this problem because learners also differ in their willingness to use this option. Another option is to penalise wrong answers, but this may affect women differently from men (Coffman & Klinowski, 2020). If a learner is willing to guess on completely unfamiliar items, they have a one in four chance of making a correct guess. It is not a good idea to apply a guessing correction to the total score in a vocabulary size test, for example reducing the total score by 25% or some other figure to account of possible guessing. The words sampled for inclusion in a vocabulary size test should represent an appropriate range of frequencies, and there is

a reasonably close connection between word frequency and likelihood of a word being known. An analysis of the scores on the Vocabulary Size Test sat by native-speakers show high scores on the most frequent items and decreasingly lower scores as the frequency level decreases. Any correction factor for guessing on the Vocabulary Size Test would need to be applied only on lower frequency levels and would need to take account of the likely vocabulary size of the test-taker. It is not easy to separate guessing completely unfamiliar items from using partial sub-conscious knowledge to answer correctly. If the person using the test wants to give credit for partial knowledge, then there is the risk of including guessed unknown answers. Guessing can be controlled to some degree by the instructions given and by making sure the test does not contain large numbers of unknown words.

4. Test administration: Coxhead, Nation, Woods, and Sim (2018) compared one-on-one test administration with group administration of the Vocabulary Size Test with secondary school learners. One-on-one administration involved an administrator sitting next to each test-taker encouraging them and keeping them on task. Group administration involved one administrator supervising a group of ten or more learners as they sat the test. For low proficiency learners, one-on-one administration resulted in scores 20% higher than when the same learners sat a group administered test. This affected around one-third of the learners sitting the test. Individual administration of a test is essential for at-risk learners.
5. Complicated test items: Some multiple-choice test items have long choices that require considerable reading and decision-making. Good trialling, item analysis and test-editing should get rid of these items.
6. Self-confidence: In our secondary and adult Vocabulary Size Test studies, people who believed that they would score poorly on the test or that they had poor vocabulary knowledge would actively avoid taking the test if they could. Conversely, people who believed that they potentially had a large vocabulary were very happy to take the test.

Adults

Adults who willingly sit a vocabulary size test are likely to take it seriously. The Yes/No format and the multiple-choice format work well with adults. When using a Yes/No test with pseudo-words, the test-takers should know that some of the words are pseudo-words, and they should be clear about what a Yes response means, namely that they could provide some rough kind of meaning for the word if asked to. If prevalence data is applied to the sequencing of items in a test so that the words that are more likely to be known come first, instead of using pseudo-words, a strategy like that suggested by Diack could be used where test-takers do electronic look-up of the last words they said they knew.

Age of adult test-takers may affect the effectiveness of different formats. Bowles and Salthouse (2008) compared four different vocabulary test formats – multiple-choice synonyms, multiple-choice antonyms, recall the definition and picture identification – with a large group of adults ranging from 18 to 98 years old. All the test formats clearly measured vocabulary knowledge. The picture identification test produced the highest scores, followed by meaning-recall, and then synonyms and opposites. Scores on the picture test increased the most sharply across age. There was a decline in all test format scores from the mid-60s. Bowles and Salthouse suggest using more than one vocabulary item format if investigating vocabulary knowledge in detail, but suggest the multiple-choice synonym format if only one measure can be used. Verhaeghen's (2003) meta-analysis also favours a multiple-choice test format for older native-speakers, rather than meaning recall. Older adults may know more words, but they may need some support in accessing them. A meaning-recognition format provides this support.

Vocabulary size test measures and their administration need to take account of the age and motivation of the test-takers they are used with. They also need to take account of the purposes of testing, particularly regarding the minimum strength of knowledge that the researcher is prepared to accept as evidence of knowing a word.

CHAPTER 10

Creating a vocabulary size test

In this book we have looked at a range of vocabulary size tests of varying degrees of quality. The history of vocabulary size testing has almost as many examples of very poorly designed tests as well designed tests. In this chapter, we try to learn from the good and bad examples of the past, from experience in creating word lists, and from research in vocabulary testing to come up with a series of steps that are likely to result in a well-designed vocabulary test.

The steps involved in measuring vocabulary size

The steps involved in developing a measure of vocabulary size are as follows.

Deciding who will be tested and why

1. *Decide what age range of native-speakers will sit the test*

A clear message from the past and from common-sense is that one vocabulary measure will not be suitable for native-speakers of all ages. The most difficult native-speakers to investigate are the very young. The vocabulary of very young children tends to be idiosyncratic and reflects the evolving nature of their control of the language. In addition, very young children have their own agendas and these do not readily fit in with what an investigating adult may wish to do. Current research largely relies on productive measures of vocabulary knowledge and productive measures will underestimate what very young learners can understand and will be affected by a range of other factors that make it difficult to estimate vocabulary size. At the very least, counts of the productive vocabulary of very young children need to involve controls over the number of tokens involved, the variety of topics covered, the quality of support provided during the spoken interaction, and the degree of intrusion felt during the data-gathering. It may be possible to analyse the spoken output in more sophisticated ways using vocabulary profiling which compares the words to ranked lists of increasingly more advanced vocabulary. Vocabulary profiling has largely been done with non-native-speakers of English at secondary school or higher. Vocabulary profiling of very young native-speakers would require access to lists of words gathered from a corpus of very young native-speaker talk. A large enough corpus of children's spoken language does not yet exist. It may be possible to make usable lists from other spoken corpora because the lists involved would be unlikely to be larger than 2000 word types and would involve a limited range of topics.

Young native-speakers aged three or above seem to be capable of being tested using part of the Peabody Picture Vocabulary Test (see Farkas & Beron, 2004). If the Peabody Picture Vocabulary Test works for children of that age, then the Picture Vocabulary Size Test should also work. The advantage of the Picture Vocabulary Size test is that raw scores can be converted to vocabulary size scores. The disadvantage of the test is that it only tests up to the most frequent 6000 words of English and so has a ceiling effect for learners aged seven or eight and above. There may be value in extending the range of vocabulary covered by the Picture Vocabulary Size Test.

When native-speakers can read and talk about the meanings of words, then the range of test options becomes greater, and age becomes less of an issue when considering *how* to test. Age still remains an important consideration in *what* to test.

2. *Decide on the purpose of the test*

Vocabulary size tests are designed to measure how many words learners know. However, the item format should take account of whether we want to measure receptive or productive knowledge and whether we want to measure spoken or written knowledge. By default, most tests measure written receptive knowledge, but this decision should be considered carefully with thought given to what the results of the test will be used for. If the test results are to be used to guide a teaching and learning intervention, then there could be value in choosing a test format such as multiple-choice that gives credit for partial knowledge.

Deciding what will be measured

3. *Decide on the kind of vocabulary knowledge that you want to measure and write a description of this kind of knowledge and why it is important to measure it.*

Most vocabulary size tests measure receptive knowledge of the written form of a word and knowledge of its meaning. This knowledge is central to knowing a word. In the field of testing English as a foreign language, there has been debate over the importance of a test measuring knowledge that represents some kind of ability to make use of the language, for example, to know a word well enough to be able to recall its meaning when it is met in a reading text (Read, 2000). It is argued that the minimum knowledge needed to answer a multiple-choice test is not enough to recall the meaning of a word when it is met in reading. Meaning-recall tests, on the other hand, more closely represent this kind of knowledge. Meaning-recall tests however are difficult to administer when first language knowledge is being tested and usually require individually administered tests. It could be argued that Yes/No tests are a kind of meaning-recall test because choices are not provided, and if the test-taker is honest and consistent in following the instructions, then they require meaning recall. The use of pseudo-words in Yes/No tests provides a kind of check on honesty and consistency. The use of scales when answering (D'Anna, Zechmeister, & Hall, 1991) or self-checking (Diack, 1975b) are other ways of trying to control honesty and consistency. If multiple-choice is chosen as the means of testing, then over-estimation of vocabulary size needs to be considered as a possibility when looking at the results.

4. *Decide and justify what will be considered as words. This involves deciding what will be considered as words to measure and what will not be considered as words. It also involves considering the unit of counting, that is, what will be considered as members of a word family.*

It is best to sample the vocabulary for vocabulary size tests from word lists rather than dictionaries. This avoids the methodological errors described in Chapter 3. Using word lists also makes the decisions about what will be considered as words and as members of word families more transparent. It is important that decisions about words and family members are made independently of existing lists. The Brysbaert, Stevens, Mandera, and Keuleers (2016) study is an excellent example of this. Although word lists were available, they considered that the BNC/COCA lists had too conservative a definition of word family because those lists only used families built on free-form stems. Brysbaert et al. rightly considered that adult native-speakers had more developed morphological skills than that and thus wanted to use a more inclusive definition of word family. They also wanted to test both the most inclusive definition and one of the least inclusive definitions of word families (flemmas) so that they could see the size of the effects of the extreme definitions on vocabulary test results.

The BNC/COCA lists include lists of words that would not normally be included in a vocabulary size test (Nation, 2016). These are lists of marginal words, transparent compound words, proper names, and acronyms. A list of foreign words not yet seen as being part of English is also being developed. Each of these lists of words has their own problems. Marginal words is a catch-all category which includes exclamations, representations of sounds showing feelings or emotions (aaah, argh, brrr, hmm, psst), swear words and offensive words, and letters of the alphabet. Exclamations etc. usually have variable spellings. Swear words and offensive words are included as marginal words because they would cause offense to some people if included in a test for school children. Having lists of such words provides some indication of how many there are and thus how much their exclusion from tests affects a measure of vocabulary size. Marginal words could be included in vocabulary size tests with variable spellings being included as members of the same family. By a rough estimate based on the list of marginal words created for the BNC/COCA lists, there are between 100 to 150 such word families.

Transparent compounds are words made up of words already in the word lists where the meaning of the compound word is largely the meaning of its parts. The test for a transparent compound is to see if the meaning of the word can be expressed through using its parts, for example, a swordsman is a man who uses a sword. Here are examples of transparent compounds – *wraparound, freethinker, bedroom, snakebite, sunblock*. Transparent compounds may have variable spelling in that they may sometimes be written as one word or with a hyphen or as two words separated by a space. The main justification for not including them in a test of vocabulary size is that especially for native-speakers of English, they do not represent new learning of the same type and magnitude as learning a new word form and a new concept. Compound words that are not transparent (*spokeswoman, blowtorch, cliffhanger, brainstorm, bulkhead*) should be included in vocabulary size tests because they involve learning that is similar to learning a new word. We do not know how many such words exist in English, possibly a few thousand.

Proper names make up a very large and ever-growing class of words. Proper names of people are not included in tests of vocabulary size because they change their meaning in that many different people can have the same first name or family name. Proper names of people do however carry some constant meaning. Some first names are typically male names or female names. Some names indicate ethnic or national origin although this is now a very unreliable sign. The names of some well-known people such as Gandhi, Mandela, Einstein, Marx, Mao, Hitler, King involve a lot of background knowledge and could be included in a vocabulary size test. Proper names of countries, cities and towns, seas and oceans, continents, languages, events, religions and beliefs, and ethnic groups may also require degrees of background knowledge and could also be considered a legitimate part of vocabulary knowledge. The amount of difficult decision-making involved and the difficulties of avoiding cultural bias make it very attractive to simply avoid including proper names. A lot of proper names are also multiword units (*the Pacific Ocean, Albert Einstein, Martin Luther King*) and excluding multiword proper names but including single word proper names would be a big inconsistency. Although it seems safer to avoid including proper names in tests of vocabulary size, and it is a decision that most people would understand, not including proper names means that test-takers do not get credit for a lot of a certain kind of vocabulary learning. There are thousands and thousands of proper names.

Acronyms are words made from the first letters of several words. *WHO* stands for *World Health Organisation. Laser* stands for *light amplification by stimulated emission of radiation*, although very few people remember that. Some acronyms like *laser* are probably no longer seen as acronyms and are properly considered as normal words. Many acronyms work within the text they occur in as a short way of referring to a phrase that is mentioned often in the text. They are temporarily learned while reading the text, but may be of little value outside that text. In other texts, the same acronym may have a completely different meaning. *STD* can refer to a *sexually transmitted disease, subscriber toll dialling, a Doctor of Sacred Theology*, or *São Tomé and Principe dobra*. Some acronyms are very well known and well established, and there is justification for including those in a vocabulary size test (*DNA, BYO, FYI, RSVP, RIP, FAQ*), particularly those that are now regarded as words in their own right. Most acronyms are so transitory or variable that they are best not included in a test.

Homonyms are words that have the same spoken and written form but completely different meanings. Most homonyms have no etymological relationship. Here are some very frequent examples – *bowl* (the ball)-*bowl* (of fruit), *bridge* (across a river)-*bridge* (card game), *rest* (in a bed)-*rest* (what remains). Homonyms and homographs (words with the same written form but different spoken forms and different meanings) make up a large number of words in English (around 10% of English vocabulary) and should be included in vocabulary size tests. See Nation (2016 Chapter 3) for a more detailed discussion of homonyms. Because the majority of homonyms have one meaning that is much more common than its other meaning(s), the inclusion of homonyms in a test however requires a test item type that will direct test-takers to the tested meaning. This may require a context sentence for the tested word. Homonymy and polysemy are part of a continuum with some polysemes eventually becoming homonyms when they have moved far enough apart in meaning.

Polysemes are different related senses of the same word. We can use *foot* to refer to a part of the body or part of a hill or mountain. A *head* can be the head of a school or a bed. These different senses of a word share an underlying meaning. Dictionaries distinguish different senses of words and sometimes have different entries for some senses. When Dale and O'Rourke (1981) tested the Living Word Vocabulary, they tested several different senses of some words. Different senses are still the same word. It is no accident that we use the form *foot* for both parts of the body and parts of hills. We use the same form because we see a meaning connection. Seeing this meaning connection is what we have to do every time we use language. We use the word *foot* to refer to a baby's foot, an adult's foot, your foot, my foot, a horse's foot and so on. What dictionaries classify as different senses of a word are not different words from the viewpoint of a native-speaker. Some senses may surprise us when we first meet them, for example *That's sweet* or *Sweet as* to refer to something we are happy with, but we do not need to learn the sense as if it was a new word. If learners have trouble with polysemes in tests, that may be more a problem with the test than with the test-taker.

Some vocabulary size test makers deliberately exclude technical words (Brysbaert et al., 2016; Diack, 1975b). The decision about what is technical is usually not done on the basis of criteria (see Chung & Nation, 2004 for an example of using criteria), but is left to the decisions that dictionary-makers made when compiling a particular dictionary. In this context, the term *technical word* means a word that is unlikely to be known by someone not specializing in a particular field. Some fields like botany, chemistry and medicine have very large technical vocabularies which may consist of close to ten thousand words. Other fields have much smaller technical vocabularies of around a few hundred to 2000 words. Technical words are properly part of an individual's vocabulary but there is difficulty in including them in a vocabulary size test. To be fair, all technical vocabularies would need to be sampled from in a test and this would make the test rather large and the test would include a lot of items that most people sitting the test would not know. It would be good to have some criteria that would provide a consistent basis for excluding technical words. The idea of prevalence (likelihood of being known) could be a useful way to approach the problem, particularly for the very low frequency words where frequency figures are uniformly low. The availability of prevalence figures (Brysbaert, Mandera, McCormick, & Keuleers, 2019) could be used to order these very low frequency items.

Words from other languages are typically not included in vocabulary size tests. Words from other languages are increasingly borrowed into most languages and the problem is drawing the line between when a word is no longer seen as a foreign word but as a legitimate word in the language. There is also the issue, when talking more generally about an individual's vocabulary size, of including vocabulary from other languages that the individual speaks or reads.

Measures of vocabulary size typically measure knowledge of single words. However, especially in the teaching of English as a foreign language, there has been growing interest in knowledge of multiword units such as *as well, by and large, raining cats and dogs, in the nick of time, multiparty talks,* and *at the end of the day*. Should multiword units be included in vocabulary size tests along with single words? The issue involved in answering this question is similar to the issue involved in dealing with polysemes. Are multiword units truly like new words for a native-speaker or do native-speakers deal with multiword units in a different way from single words by considering their parts? There is only a small number of core idioms in English, less than 100, where the meaning of the parts does not contribute to the meaning of the whole (Grant & Nation, 2006), but it is better to be consistent in a test and stick to single words.

5. *Bearing in mind your decisions at steps 1 and 2, choose or develop a list of words. This list needs to be large enough and representative enough to make sure that all the words that are part of the test-takers' knowledge occur in the list.*

There are now lists of words freely available using various definitions of word family. These include Nation's BNC/COCA lists <https://www.wgtn.ac.nz/lals/resources/vocabulary-analysis-programs> and Brysbaert et al.'s (2016) lemma and word family lists <https://www.frontiersin.org/article/10.3389/fpsyg.2016.01116> or <https://www.researchgate.net/profile/Marc_Brysbaert>. These lists have been crosschecked and while there are some minor discrepancies, the cross-checking shows that there are few serious omissions from the lists. The main reason for creating new lists would be to use a different level of word family.

6. *Check your word list to make sure that there are no serious omissions and errors.*

Word lists can be checked against each other and can be run over large corpora to make sure that no important words are missing from the lists. The AntWordProfiler program, freely available at <www.laurenceanthony.net/software/antwordprofiler>, is useful for doing these jobs.

7. *Sample a suitable number of words from the list so that the sample is a good representation of the whole list and so that the total number of words in the sample is large enough to obtain a good level of reliability and small enough to be able to be tested within a sensible testing time.*

Brysbaert et al., (2016) provided a different sample of words for each person sitting the test so that eventually all words in their list were tested several times. This was because one of their goals was to create prevalence norms for all the words. Their use of a Yes/No format helped make this possible. If a different test format was used, such as multiple-choice, then a sample of words may need to be used. Usually it is a good idea to make several equivalent samples at the same time so that there can be several equivalent forms of the test. This helps in maintaining test security.

If the test is going to be used as a measure of total vocabulary size, then a sample size of 100 words is easily enough for good reliability (Beglar, 2010). If only parts of the test are likely to be used with younger native-speakers, then enough words need to be sampled so that the partial test has enough words for good reliability.

Deciding how to measure whether a word is known

8. *Bearing in mind your decisions at steps 1 and 2, decide on a test-item type and justify your decision.*

Chapter 9 looked at various item types. The choice of an item type is affected by a variety of factors including the age of the test-takers, the purpose of the test, the attitudes of the test-takers, the need to gather other data besides size, the time available for testing, the need for individual testing, and the method of scoring the test. For learners of English as a foreign language, there is a validity advantage in using a recall item-type. For native-speakers, managing and scoring a recall item-type is much more difficult because translations cannot be used as responses. If native-speakers use the Yes/No item-type in the way it should be used, genuinely determining if they could provide a meaning for each tested word, then it could be argued that the Yes/No item type is a kind of meaning-recall item. It is likely that putting each word in a short non-defining context sentence might make this work, but that requires research on this item-type.

The reason for including a justification of the item type is to make sure that the choice of item type is well thought out, and to make it clear to users of the test what is being measured.

9. *Make the test.*

Making Yes/No tests requires computing skills. Making multiple-choice tests requires clear, well-thought-out guidelines and frequent discussion amongst the writers of the item types. When making equivalent forms, it is important that enough items for all forms are made at the same time to ensure that the same guidelines are applied to the choice of distractors and the writing of the context sentence and choices. If a recall format is being used, then the beginnings of criteria for correct answers need to be developed that will be added to and adapted as the test is trialed and used.

10. *Thoroughly check, trial, and gather data on the performance of the test and the test items, making changes to the test where necessary.*

Pilot testing is a feature of well-planned research. Careful preparation can avoid a lot of problems before they have a chance to occur. There are formal measures (item analysis) to check the items in a test including Rasch analysis. However, before these more formal checks are applied, it is helpful to do several bits of informal checking to improve the test. Here are some suggestions.

If non-defining context sentences are used, run the sentences through the AntWordProfiler program to make sure that the context words used are high frequency words. Get someone to read the context sentences to make sure they make sense and do not contain errors. Make any necessary changes, and then get someone else to do the same again. Put pseudo-words in place of the test words in the context sentence and see if someone can guess the tested word. If they can, you may need to change the sentence, because it is directing the test-takers to the right answer.

If choices are used, the choices need be written to appropriate guidelines, and then need to be checked to make sure that they meet the guidelines, are comprehensible, and are not obviously giving away the correct answer. The distractors should be the meanings of words that are at the same frequency or familiarity level as the tested word. The choices should be written using words that are more frequent or more familiar than the words being tested. Running the test through AntWordProfiler can help check this. Several individuals should check the test, not at the same time but one after other, so that each person's suggested changes can be considered and incorporated before the next person checks it. An interesting way of checking is to blank out the test word and see if the correct choice can be made without seeing the test word. Having someone do a think-aloud while sitting the test is also a valuable way of improving the test. The main point is that the early stages of checking the test should not involve a large group of people sitting the test, but should involve getting rid of obvious errors and gathering good quality data from a few people. After this intensive preparatory checking, groups of people can be used to gather statistical data to make sure that the test is performing well.

Estimating vocabulary size from the test results

11. *Use the test to gather data from a suitable population and estimate vocabulary sizes by multiplying the score on the test by ratio of the sample to the whole list.*

These steps can be applied to a variety of different kinds of vocabulary size tests. Following a series of steps is similar to using a checklist. It makes sure that all the necessary factors are considered.

CHAPTER 11

Needed research and some final thoughts

The number of methodologically-sound data-gathering studies that focus on the measurement of the total vocabulary size of native-speakers of English can be counted on one hand. Fortunately, these studies together cover a good range of age levels. Research on English word lists has given a reasonably clear indication of the extent of the number of words in the language (the size of the ball-park) we are working with, and we now have some understanding of the factors affecting the measurement of vocabulary size, particularly the degree of inclusiveness of the word family, and what we should count as words. The size of the ball-park is a very important piece of knowledge because most of the earlier vocabulary size studies got this very wrong. The size of the ball-park sets the upper limit for vocabulary size, and once that is known, the average growth in vocabulary size is largely predictable by Heaps Law, and individual variation around the average is affected by a range of economic, social and personal factors.

It is important to realize the value of knowing the size of the ball-park. The Oxford English Dictionary is said to contain over a million words, but when we look closely at this, it is clear that this does not mean one million different word families. It seems to mean entries in the dictionary, and these entries include several entries for the same word, multiword units, and archaic words. The number of word families that make-up the general vocabulary of modern English is much less than 50,000. The inclusion of technical words of all fields might double this number, but no native-speaker ends up knowing every word in English. Knowing the size of the ball-park allows us to have realistic views of the size of the vocabulary learning task facing young native-speakers and learners of English as a second or foreign language. The basic rule of thumb of 1000 word families a year or around three word families per day makes it clear that well-thought-out interventions to boost vocabulary size could have a noticeable effect. Such interventions seem even more feasible when we realize that the occurrence of the vocabulary of English follows Zipf's Law, namely that high frequency words and mid-frequency words (Nation, 2013; Schmitt & Schmitt, 2014) account for a very high percentage of the running words (tokens) in spoken and written uses of the language. In other words, focusing on the most useful, as yet unknown, words of the language with young native-speakers could have substantial effects on language use.

It is important to see vocabulary-focused interventions as involving much more than vocabulary teaching. While vocabulary teaching has its uses, particularly in the context of learning a new subject area, vocabulary teaching is largely inefficient and only moderately effective (see Carlo et al. (2004) for a particularly inefficient vocabulary teaching intervention). Vocabulary learning occurs across the four strands of meaning-focused input, meaning-focused output, language-focused learning, and fluency development (Nation, 2007a). Teaching is only a small part of language-focused learning, and there also need to be interventions involving (1) spoken interaction as in shared-book reading, problem-solving discussions, and discovery learning, (2) substantial amounts of extensive reading and listening, and (3) developing word consciousness and vocabulary learning strategies such as dictionary use and word part analysis.

Vocabulary growth

One way of visualizing vocabulary growth is to see it as being like a tree. The high-frequency vocabulary of around 3000 word families represents the roots. Without these, no real communication is possible. The 6000 mid-frequency word families represent the trunk. While the high-frequency and mid-frequency words are being learned, largely but not exclusively through spoken input, low-frequency words are being added through hobbies, specialised interests, and later jobs. The various groupings of low frequency words are the branches of the tree. The branches rely on the roots and the trunk. Some branches develop early low down the trunk. These may represent children's obsessions with things such as dinosaurs, horses or some other animal, video-games, and sport. School subjects provide opportunities for other branches to develop. Some branches may be small because they involve areas where the unique technical vocabulary is small. Others may be large. The substantial high branches of the tree relate to subjects studied at secondary school and university, to occupations and professions, and to major interests outside of study and work. The branches head in various directions and very much represent choices and the unplanned opportunities that occur in life.

Each person's vocabulary tree has a predictable set of roots and trunk, and some of the branches are predictable in a particular country's educational system and culture. Even native-speakers with very limited opportunities in life learn the high-frequency and mid-frequency vocabulary represented by the roots and trunk, and largely learn it in a roughly predictable order, which in large part is determined by word-family frequency.

The evidence to support the analogy of the tree comes from studies of word frequency and word prevalence (Biemiller, 2005, 2010; Dale & O'Rourke, 1976,

1981; Brysbaert, Mandera, McCormick, & Keuleers, 2019), vocabulary size testing (Coxhead, Nation, & Sim, 2015; Coxhead, Nation, Woods, & Sim, 2018), vocabulary coverage (Nation, 2016; Schmitt & Schmitt, 2014), and technical vocabulary (Chung & Nation, 2004). The frequency and prevalence studies show a predictable order for high-frequency and mid-frequency words (Biemiller, 2010). Vocabulary size testing shows that by the age of 13 or 14, even the native-speakers scoring lowest on vocabulary size tests know around 9000 words, and even native-speakers who are barely literate know most of the first 9000 words. The vocabulary coverage studies show the general service nature of the high-frequency words (they occur in all kinds of uses of the language), and the need to know the mid-frequency vocabulary as well in order to cope with the demands of listening, movie and TV watching, and daily reading. The technical vocabulary studies show that each technical area has a specialised vocabulary, and the size and uniqueness of this specialised vocabulary differs greatly from one subject area to another. In some subject areas such as medicine, the vocabulary unique to that subject area makes up a large proportion of the technical vocabulary of that area and also consists of many thousand words. In other subject areas, such as applied linguistics, the unique specialized vocabulary is a relatively small part of the total technical vocabulary of the area, and the total technical vocabulary may be 1000 words or less.

The vocabulary gap

The studies showing a vocabulary gap between young high-socio-economic and low-socio-economic learners are worrying, because they particularly concern high-frequency words, the roots of the tree, which every native-speaker will soon learn, even if some experience a lag. Even in environments where some young native-speakers receive much less input than their peers, there should still be more than enough repetitions of high-frequency words to ensure learning. The critical difference affecting the rate of vocabulary growth must therefore lie in the quality of the interactions between care-givers and children and the variety of topics rather than the quantity of input. Another possibility is that our measurement of vocabulary knowledge is at fault, and that the differences we see in young native-speaking children's knowledge of high-frequency words is at least partially a measurement problem. It is important to investigate this issue, because if there is a measurement problem then this will affect the effectiveness of any interventions. A hidden measurement problem may result in us focusing on vocabulary that is already well-enough known and neglecting vocabulary that truly deserves attention. There is some evidence that this occurs in interventions with teen-age native-speakers (Nation, 2007b).

Let us now suggest further useful pieces of future research.

1. Developing research tools

Researching vocabulary size involves using some test or measure of vocabulary knowledge. Although we now have freely available tests, they can be improved and added to.

A picture test of total vocabulary size

The Peabody Picture Vocabulary Test (Dunn, 1965) has been a staple of vocabulary growth research for over fifty years. It is not a test of total vocabulary size, but the development of the Picture Vocabulary Size Test has shown that it is possible to make a picture-based test that draws on a randomly chosen representative sample of words. The Peabody Picture Vocabulary Test is based on an opportunistically chosen sample of words that does not allow any generalization beyond that sample. The Picture Vocabulary Size Test could be extended to be a test of total vocabulary size drawing on the BNC/COCA lists that could be used with a wide range of native-speakers not only to compare groups and individuals but to also say something about the total number of words known. This would take vocabulary size research forward in a very productive way.

Refining the BNC/COCA lists

The BNC/COCA lists are the most extensive, carefully made lists of word families that can be drawn on for measures of vocabulary size. The division of words into sub-lists is based on range and frequency figures. Brysbaert, Mandera, McCormick, & Keuleers (2019) have provided prevalence figures that can be used to improve the sequencing of words and sub-lists so that vocabulary size tests based on the lists can be more sensibly shortened to avoid testing words that the test-takers are not likely to know. Such lists would also be valuable in developing computer-adaptive vocabulary size tests.

2. Improving the methodology of vocabulary size research

The methodology of vocabulary size research has improved in recent years but there are still issues that need clearing up.

How can we determine the optimal size of a word family for native-speakers of various ages?

Do vocabulary size tests need to have special sections that target topic areas relating to study, employment, and hobbies?
How can we standardize the support given to test-takers when taking a vocabulary size test?
Can we triangulate test performance with motivation and/or test-taking strategy surveys to provide a way of substantiating the factors affecting performance on a vocabulary size test?
Does the format of a meaning-recall test have a substantial effect on the scores? What are the different effects of cued written recall as in Laufer and Goldstein (2004) versus any form of written recall (in addition to the option of cued recall) versus oral interview?
Should credit be given for partial knowledge in a meaning-recall test?
Can prevalence figures be used to sequence items in a test and is such sequencing useful for measuring vocabulary size?

3. Answering research questions on native-speaker vocabulary size and growth

Because there has been so little research on total vocabulary size, there are many research questions that remain unanswered.

The rate of vocabulary growth

We know very little about the rate of growth in vocabulary size. Some of the following questions have been addressed in the research literature, but the research on them needs replicating and refining.

How much vocabulary do young native-speakers know when they begin primary school? How much do children of the same age differ from each other?
Do young children have a large enough vocabulary size to begin learning to read?
Do children born in an English-speaking country who live in homes where more than one language is spoken have vocabulary sizes comparable to those of native-speakers from monolingual English-speaking homes?
Does learning to read result in a sharp increase in vocabulary size? How soon after learning to read can we see the effects of reading on vocabulary growth?
Do learners of the same age from different socio-economic groups have comparable vocabulary sizes?
At what rate do young immigrants to an English-speaking country pick up English vocabulary?

How wide is the range of vocabulary sizes at each age level? What are the likely causes of this variation?
When does the rough rule of thumb of an increase of roughly 1000 words a year no longer apply?
Does university study result in a sharp increase in vocabulary size?
Do we see similar increases in size when young adults enter employment?

The effects of interventions on vocabulary size growth

Is the amount of reading done directly related to vocabulary size growth or are there limits to the effects of reading on vocabulary size?
Are interventions focused on variety of experience more effective in increasing vocabulary size than interventions focused on quantity of input or quality of interaction?

4. Using the data from vocabulary size tests

Vocabulary size tests provide us with estimates of vocabulary size, but we need to know what these estimates mean, especially in terms of language skills and opportunities to benefit from education.

Can a learner with meaning-recognition knowledge of a word deal effectively with that word in reading or listening even though they cannot correctly answer a meaning-recall test of the word?
Does a recall test set the knowledge requirement for reading or listening too high?
Do vocabulary size measures predict educational performance? At what age does vocabulary size become important?

The future of vocabulary size testing

Computerization and the internet have had striking effects on the measurement of native-speaker vocabulary size. The availability of corpus analysis tools and substantial corpora has allowed us to develop and refine word lists which in their various forms are at the core of vocabulary size measurement. The internet has allowed testing of very large numbers of people.

So far, computer-adaptive testing has not been applied to vocabulary size testing, but given the large numbers of words available for testing and the availability of frequency data and prevalence data for stratifying and sequencing words and groups of words, the time seems ripe for developing computer-adaptive total-vocabulary-size tests.

The most pleasing aspect of vocabulary size measurement has been the growing consensus around the number of words in English and the number of words that native-speakers know. After the bizarre estimates of vocabulary size and growth made in the middle of the twentieth century, it is good to see sanity returning to the field.

APPENDIX 1

Instructions for individual test administration for research assistants

(Coxhead, Nation, Woods, & Sim, 2018)

Procedure

1. Sit next to the person doing the test so that you can see the screen. ONLY TEST ONE PERSON AT A TIME. This is because it is essential that the person sitting the test gives it their full attention, is personally encouraged to keep trying, and is helped if the pronunciation of any words is needed.
2. Provide support and encouragement in any or all of the following ways that you see as being appropriate. Pilot testing has revealed that a learner who sits the test with someone like you sitting next to them and encouraging them gets much higher scores than someone sitting the test without the support.
   i. Say "Good" after each item is done. If the learner wants feedback on correctness, provide the answer after they have completed the item.
   ii. Encourage the learner to rest after doing several levels of items. You could use this time to get feedback on how they view the test, and to confirm and check items on the background form.
   iii. If the learner is uncertain about an item, encourage them to guess. For many items, learners will have only a vague idea of their meaning and this knowledge may even be subconscious. Where possible encourage informed strategic guessing, but discourage what is obviously random guessing. Overall, however, it is better to guess than not guess.
   iv. If you think a learner has problems reading a word, read it aloud for them. The vocabulary size test is a test of receptive knowledge of vocabulary, but this does not have to be limited to reading.
   v. If you think that the learner is not sitting the test properly, or if you have any reason to doubt the accuracy of their performance, let us know. In some cases you may decide to abandon the administration to a particular learner if you feel the result will not truly reflect their knowledge. Be sure to keep some notes about this if you do.
   vi. It is important that the learner tries all items on the test if this is at all possible. Typically learners know some very low-frequency words.
3. Please note any comments you have about the test, about the learner, or about the learners sitting of the test. We want the results to reflect the learners' knowledge as closely as possible.

APPENDIX 2

Vocabulary size test feedback sheet for scores over 10,000 words

(Coxhead, Nation, Woods, & Sim, 2018)

Victoria
UNIVERSITY OF WELLINGTON
Te Whare Wānanga
o te Ūpoko o te Ika a Māui

Vocabulary Size Test Feedback
Over 10,000 words

Thanks for taking this vocabulary size test. This is a test of your receptive vocabulary, meaning the knowledge of words you have for reading and listening. Generally speaking, if we count from when a native-speaker is two or three years old, their vocabulary size increases by 1,000 words per year. For second language learners, this rate is not so fast. Your vocabulary size is over 10,000 words, which indicates that it is more than enough for university studies. If you want to increase it, you could try these things:

1. Increase the amount of reading you do every day.
2. Read widely. For example, you could read newspapers online from NZ and other countries, non-fiction books on topics that interest you, and magazines such as the Listener or the Economist, and your textbooks too.
3. Listen widely and often. For example, you could listen to Radio New Zealand National programs on radio or as podcasts, watch information rich programs on tv like documentaries, and talk about the content and ideas of these programs with friends and family.
4. Concentrate on the technical vocabulary of your subjects.
5. Use activities such as word cards to keep track of words you want to learn and revise these words often. Pay attention to the spelling of words, as well as common patterns they occur in.
6. Try to introduce words you recognise but don't use often into your speaking and writing. Seek feedback on your use of these words from other people.
7. Look for examples of words being used in different contexts. Note them down (on word cards or in a notebook, for example) and focus on learning their meaning.

APPENDIX 3

Thorndike, E. L. (1924). The vocabularies of school pupils. In J. C. Bell (Ed.), *Contributions to Education* (pp. 69–76). New York, NY: World Book Co.

This article is reproduced here in its entirety because it is such a difficult article to find and it is the most important early discussion of vocabulary size testing methodology. Its inclusion should also be seen as a recognition of the tremendous work done by Edward Thorndike in the development of word lists, the measurement of vocabulary knowledge and the teaching and learning of vocabulary.

THE VOCABULARIES OF SCHOOL PUPILS

Edward L. Thorndike

Teachers College, Columbia University

It would seem to be a very simple matter to find out how many words pupils of a given age or school grade know, but there is a very wide diversity among the estimates made by those who have studied the matter. In this article I shall review the previous investigations, point out certain principles of method, and show the limits between which the truth probably lies, with special reference to the word-knowledge of pupils in Grade 9.

Kirkpatrick, Doran, Babbitt, Bonser, Gerlach, Brandenburg, Terman, Neher, and Holley have estimated the number of words known by testing individuals with a sample list chosen from some dictionary, and then multiplying the numbers that the individual new by $\frac{n \text{ in dictionary}}{n \text{ in sample}}$.

The tests used have been (*a*) to check the words known, (*b*) to define them, (*c*) to use them in sentences, and (*d*) to select the right meaning from alternatives.

Kirkpatrick ('07) used a list of 100 words selected from Webster's Academic Dictionary. The subjects were given a printed list and were asked to mark the words they knew with a plus (+) sign, those they did not know with a minus (–) sign, and doubtful ones with a question mark. There was the added direction to "count as known all the words that you would not, as to their meanings, need to look up in the dictionary if you saw them in a sentence." The resulting estimates are shown in Table 1.

Doran ('07) reports that he used word lists varying from one thousand to several thousand words, and required written or oral definitions. He selected all words on a page, except such unusual words as hardly anybody would know and selected the pages either at random, or more often in a certain order, as every twenty-fifth or fiftieth page. In school No. 1

(The end of page 69)

and in the normal school, he used Webster's High School Dictionary; in school No. 2, he used Webster's International. In the latter school the tests were given at intervals for two or three

Table 1. Estimates of Range of Vocabulary of the Average Pupil of Certain Grades or Mental Ages

Grade	Kirkpatrick	Doran		Bonser						Brandenburg	Gerlach	Neher	Holley (est.)	Terman
		Dict 1	Dict 2	Dict A			Dict B							
				School A	School A	School B	School C	School D	School E					
2	4480									4000				
3	6620									5429			3144	M.A.8 3600
4	7020			10886						6887			5220	
5	7860			13216	21648	17600	17952	19404	24904	8207			6030	M.A10 5400
6	8700	4192	11634	17038	30184	26520				9613			7470	
7	10660	5849	13675	17052	27720					11445			8478	M.A.12 7200
8	12000	7937	17138	18704	31120					12819			9378	
9	13400		18865											
1H	13640									13504	66650	9000	10296	M.A.14 9000
2H	16020									15340		10080	10926	
3H	17600									13974		11520	11565	Av. Adult 11700
4H	18720									14975	76250	11700	11752	
Normal School	19000		15750											Superior Adult 13500
			19400											
			21500[1]											
College	20120													

1. 11700 and 15400 for low-grade classes in this normal school

months. He estimated by multiplying in the same fashion as Kirkpatrick, allowing for the unusual words. His estimates appear in Table 1.

Babbitt used Kirkpatrick's methods, with the exception that the dictionary was an unabridged one, containing over 100,000 words.

Bonser ('15) used Kirkpatrick's list in his first testing of the Speyer School. In his second test of the pupils at the Speyer School, and in his testing of pupils at Edgewater, Horace Mann, Teachers College, and elsewhere, he used a list of 150 words selected from Webster's Elementary School Dictionary, which contains 44,000 words. In both cases he used Kirkpatrick's methods. His estimates appear in Table 1.

Brandenburg ('18) used a list of 200 words, one for every 140 in Webster's Academic Dictionary. The instructions were as follows: "In the space after each word that you know, write a sentence using the word correctly. Place a cross before each word that you do not know." His estimates appear in Table 1.

Terman ('16) used a list of 100 words, selected from Laird and Lee's Vest Pocket Dictionary, containing 18,000 words, and tested pupils individually by oral definition. He estimated the number of words in the subject's vocabulary by multiplying his score in the test by 180. His estimates are for Stanford Mental Ages.

Neher ('18) used Terman's methods and also took his words from the dictionary from which Terman chose the Stanford list.

Gerlach ('17) used "the first word of the third column of every third page and thirtieth page" of Funk and Wagnalls' New Standard Dictionary, making 1000 in all. "Biographical and geographical terms were omitted." In the case of 400 of the least familiar of the thousand words, the subjects were asked to define those which they knew. Each of the remaining 600 words were supplied with four definitions, only one of which was correct. The subjects were asked to

(The end of page 71)

check the correct definitions. He estimated that his list was representative of 250,000 words. He deducted from the number of the 600 which were correctly marked, one third of the number wrongly marked, and added the number of the 400 which were correctly defined. The resulting number he multiplied by 250.

Holley ('19) used Terman's list of 100 words, the task being to select the right word from four, as in:

> A gown is a … string … animal … dress … plant.
> An orange is a … dress … animal … fruit … hornet.

He did not estimate total vocabulary, but his list is, as stated, the same as Terman's and his averages multiplied by 180 give the numbers of Table 1.

The discrepancies in the results of Table 1 taken at their face value are obviously very great. For the average first-year high school pupil, for example, we have a range from 9000 to 66,650. The same investigator reports 7937 and 17,138 for the average pupil in Grade 8, according to the school and dictionary used. Bonser, using Kirkpatrick's method, estimates 18,704 and 32,120 for Grade 8 in the same school, according to the dictionary used, whereas Kirkpatrick's result was only 12,000 or 13,400 (Grades 8 and 9, respectively, in an elementary school with a ninth-grade course).

These discrepancies are partly due to the dictionary used. For example, Terman's estimates are of how many correct definitions an individual would give if he were tested with the 18,000 words of the Laird and Lee book. They would be enormously increased if plurals, comparatives and superlatives, past tenses, and familiar derivatives are to be counted as words known. As to root words and unfamiliar derivatives, his estimates are too low if the individuals know such words that are not contained in the Laird and Lee dictionary. This is almost certainly true of the superior adult. Up to the mental age of 12, this source of error is probably nearly negligible. For his primary purpose of a test of intelligence, of course, the Laird and Lee list is satisfactory.

The discrepancies are partly due to the method of selecting

(The end of page 72)

words in a dictionary. To take a random sample of 100 words from a dictionary containing, say, 28,000, we should take words 1, 281, 561, 841, etc., or words 2, 282, 562, 842, etc., or the equivalent. Nobody, it appears, has done this. For example, Gerlach took the first word on every third page and on every thirtieth page. This or any similar method will overweight the sample with the more important words, unless the dictionary used gives equal space to all words, since the more space a word has given to it in a dictionary, the more chance it has of being the first word on a page. For example, suppose that certain words have each half a page devoted to them, and that certain other words have one fiftieth of a page devoted to them. Then the chances are one in two that one of the first set will be the first word on each page where it is, while the chances are only one in fifty for one of the second set.[1] nobody, except possibly Terman seems to have noted this factor of error, nor the corollary that in the long run the larger the dictionary used, the more the overweighting will be, since the bigger dictionaries show the greater variations in the amount of space given to different words.

Gerlach's list shows very clearly the effect of this error,[2] since his list of a thousand words supposed by him to be a random sampling of about 275,000, contains nearly a third as many words from the first 10,000 for importance as from the entire remaining 265,000 words of less importance.

Brandenburg states that his words were selected "at equal intervals throughout the dictionary." This probably means equal intervals of space, since if he had encountered off equal numbers of words defined, he would probably have given himself credit for the labor involved, and stated the reason for the expense of time. In his list of 200 words, 57 are from the

[1] This assumes that "being the first word on a page" means being the first word any part of whose definition forms the beginning of a page. If it means being the first word the beginning of whose definition is the first beginning of any definition on the page, this calculation of chances does not apply; but there is still a heavy overweighting, because important words often appear each as several words listed separately in the dictionary.

[2] It should be noted that for Gerlach's main purpose, the comparison of the sexes, the error was not important.

(The end of page 73)

first 5000 for importance approximately, and only 163 from the remaining 23,000.

It is to be hoped that future workers who estimate range of vocabulary will consider the nature of the list which they sample and the method of sampling more thoroughly than has been the case in the past.

The discrepancies are partly due to the method of the test. Pupils may quite honestly think they know a word and so check it for Kirkpatrick or Bonser, who could not define it well enough to pass Terman's test on it. Pupils may be unable to define "majesty" who could check the correct word in "Majesty, refers to … dresses … kings … countries … climates."

Both questions, "What is meant by knowing a word?" and "How many words are there in the English language?" are really very complex. We can define what by degree of knowledge we mean by the test we frame for any given word and the key for scoring the test. Terman, Gerlach, and Holley do so, and Brandenburg presumably had a key for scoring the sentences that would serve the same purpose. The selection form of test tends to represent a rather vague, inadequate, and loose knowledge, but it can be made to represent a very exacting standard, as when five distinctions are required or temptations to error are introduced, as in

habitat	dweller	bodice	prodigality	habit	home
cord	dispute	harmony	famine	firewood	string

In spite of the apparent discrepancies in the estimates of Table 1, a critical study of the original reports enables us to make an approximate estimate of the word-knowledge of the average pupil at the beginning of Grade 9, for the first year of a four-year high school course.

"To know a word" shall mean for us "to be able to define it passably, or at least recognise a definition of it among three or four wrong definitions."[1] We shall not count plurals in *s*, verbs in *s* or *d* or *ing* or *n*, past tenses in *d*, comparatives and superlatives in *or, est, r,* and *st,* or adverbs in *ly*. We shall

[1] This is lamentably vague, but is the best we can do at present.

(The end of page 74)

consider first the estimates made as a result of tests, not the opinions of individual pupils as to what they know. Terman's mental age of fourteen may be taken as nearly equivalent to the average first-year high school pupil, since the Terman mental age fourteen is probably well above the chronological fourteen-year-old of the country as a whole. His estimate of 9000 is low, since some of the pupils would know some of the words not in the Laird and Lee. Neher's 9000 for first-year high school pupils is low for the same reason. Holley's 10,296 tends to be low for this same reason, but tends to be high because his selection tests are so easy. Brandenburg's 13,500 is high because of the selection error described above, and because his criterion of use in a sentence is not at all exacting.

Gerlach's 66,650 shrinks greatly because of this error, and because the 275,000 which he tried to sample included probably many of the forms which we have ruled out. The average first-year high school pupil scored 266.6 (median 267) words on Gerlach's test of 1000. If we assume that he knew the most important 266 of the 1000, his vocabulary would be about 11,000, since 240 of the Gerlach 1000 words are in the Thorndike list of the 10,000 most important words.[1] Allowing generously for the fact that he probably knew more words outside the Thorndike list than he failed on within the list, his vocabulary would still be under 14,000. So it seems fairly certain that the number of words (excluding the forms mentioned above and compounds which are obviously understandable from their component words) which are known well enough to define them passably, is between 9500 and 12,500.

Doran's results cannot well be used, because we do not know just how to treat his allowance for the very unfamiliar words.

Our own results with the Thorndike tests are in accord with this. The median score is 65 and a test of 100 words, 76 words of which are from the Thorndike 10,000 and 24 of

[1] More than 240 are in the list, but some are used in the test with very rare meanings and so are not counted by us; e.g., bear, to force down the price of..

(The end of page 75)

which are from the next 10,000 for importance, the task of selecting synonyms being deliberately made hard by the requirement of some fine distinctions. If the words known were the most important, they would correspond to about 9000 words as a total vocabulary. Allowing for the fact that the pupils would know more outside the 1000 than they would fail on within the 10,000, we have from 10,000 to 11,500 as an estimate.[1]

Babbitt, E. H. (1907). A vocabulary test. *Popular Science Monthly, 70*, 378.

Bonser, F. G., Burch, L. H., and Turner, M. R. (1915). Vocabulary tests as measures of school efficiency. *School and Society, 2*, 713–718.

Brandenburg, T. C. (1918). Psychological aspects of language. *Journal of Educational Psychology, 9*, 313–332.

Doran, E. W. (1907). A study of vocabularies. *Pedagogical Seminary, 14*(4), 401–438.

Gerlach, F. M. (1917). Vocabulary studies. *Studies in Education and Psychology*, No. 1, Colorado College.

Holley, C. E. (1919). First Annual Report of the Bureau of Educational Research, University of Illinois.

Kirkpatrick, E. A. (1907). A vocabulary test. *Popular Science Monthly, 70*, 157–164.

Neher, H. L. (1918). Measuring the vocabulary of high school pupils. *School and Society, 8*, 355–359.

Terman, L. M. (1916). *The Measurement of Intelligence*. Boston: Houghton-Mifflin.

Thorndike, E. L. (1921). *The Teacher's Word Book*. New York: Teachers College Columbia University.

Thorndike, E. L. (1921). Word knowledge in the elementary school. *Teachers College Record, 22*, 334–370.

[1] There are many matters to be considered in such estimates, such as the allowance for chance successes in the selection form of test, the case of recognising a definition in comparison with framing one, and the allowance for the proper names which make up part of the Thorndike list of 10,000. We have had those in mind, but make no claim to rigorous or exact treatment of them. Such a treatment is hardly worthwhile with the data at hand. When we have 20,000 or more words rated for importance, and tests for each thousand or two thousand, and a rigid scoring, and perhaps tests sampling adequately the different meanings of the same word, much greater refinement of treatment will be in order.

(The end of page 76)

References

Alexander, F., & Chamberlain, I. C. (1904). Studies of a child. *Pedagogical Seminary*, 11, 263–291.

Anderson, R. C., & Freebody, P. (1983). Reading comprehension and the assessment and acquisition of word knowledge. *Advances in Reading/Language Research*, 2, 231–256.

Babbitt, E. H. (1907). A vocabulary test. *Popular Science Monthly*, 70, 378.

Banerji, N., Gupta, V., Kilgarriff, A., & Tugwell, D. (2012). *Oxford Children's Corpus: A Corpus of Children's Writing, Reading, and Education*. <https://www.sketchengine.co.uk/documentation/raw.../Beebox_final.docx>.

Barry, C. L., Horst, S. J., Finney, S. J., Brown, A. R., & Kopp, J. P. (2010). Do examinees have similar test-taking effort? A high-stakes question for low-stakes testing. *International Journal of Testing*, 10(4), 342–363. https://doi.org/10.1080/15305058.2010.508569

Bauer, L., & Nation, I. S. P. (1993). Word families. *International Journal of Lexicography*, 6(4), 253–279. https://doi.org/10.1093/ijl/6.4.253

Beglar, D. (2010). A Rasch-based validation of the Vocabulary Size Test. *Language Testing*, 27(1), 101–118. https://doi.org/10.1177/0265532209340194

Biemiller, A. (2005). Size and sequence in vocabulary development. In E. H. Hiebert & M. L. Kamil (Eds.), *Teaching and learning vocabulary: Bringing research into practice* (pp. 223–242). Mahwah, NJ: Lawrence Erlbaum Associates.

Biemiller, A. (2010). *Words worth teaching: Closing the vocabulary gap*. Columbus, OH: McGraw-Hill.

Biemiller, A., & Boote, C. (2006). An effective method for building meaning vocabulary in primary grades. *Journal of Educational Psychology*, 98, 44–62. https://doi.org/10.1037/0022-0663.98.1.44

Biemiller, A., & Slonim, N. (2001). Estimating root word vocabulary growth in normative and advantaged populations: Evidence for a common sequence of vocabulary acquisition. *Journal of Educational Psychology*, 93(3), 498–520. https://doi.org/10.1037/0022-0663.93.3.498

Bock, C. (1948). Prefixes and suffixes. *Classical Journal*, 44, 132–133.

Bohn, W. E. (1914). First steps in verbal expression. *Pedagogical Seminary*, 21, 579–595. https://doi.org/10.1080/08919402.1914.10534685

Bonser, F. G., Burch, L. H., & Turner, M. R. (1915). *Vocabulary tests as measures of school efficiency, School and Society*, 2, 713–718.

Bowles, R. P., & Salthouse, T. A. (2008). Vocabulary test format and differential relations to age. *Psychology and Aging*, 23(2), 366–376. https://doi.org/10.1037/0882-7974.23.2.366

Brandenburg, G. C. (1914). The language of a three-year-old child. *Pedagogical Seminary*, 22, 89–120. https://doi.org/10.1080/08919402.1915.10533951

Brandenburg, G. C. (1918). Psychological aspects of language. *Journal of Educational Psychology*, 9, 313–332. https://doi.org/10.1037/h0072574

Brandenburg, G. C., & Brandenburg, J. (1919). Language development during the fourth year: the conversation. *Pedagogical Seminary*, 26(1), 27–40. https://doi.org/10.1080/08919402.1919.10532620

Brown, P., & Gaskins, S. (2014). Language acquisition and language socialization. In N. J. Enfield, P. Kockelman, & J. Sidnell (Eds.), *Cambridge handbook of linguistic anthropology* (pp. 187–226). Cambridge: Cambridge University Press. https://doi.org/10.1017/CBO9781139342872

Bryan, F. E. (1953). How large are children's vocabularies? *Elementary School Journal*, 54, 210–216. https://doi.org/10.1086/458574

Brysbaert, M., Mandera, P., McCormick, S. F., & Keuleers, E. (2019). Word prevalence norms for 62,000 English lemmas. *Behavior Research Methods*, 51(2), 467–479. https://doi.org/10.3758/s13428-018-1077-9

Brysbaert, M., & New, B. (2009). Moving beyond Kucera and Francis: A critical evaluation of current word frequency norms and the introduction of a new and improved word frequency measure for American English. *Behavior Research Methods*, 41(4), 977–990. https://doi.org/10.3758/BRM.41.4.977

Brysbaert, M., Stevens, M., Mandera, P., & Keuleers, E. (2016). How many words do we know? Practical estimates of vocabulary size dependent on word definition, the degree of language input and the participant's age. *Frontiers in Psychology*, 7, 1116. https://doi.org/10.3389/fpsyg.2016.01116

Bush, A. (1914). The vocabulary of a three-year-old girl. *Pedagogical Seminary*, 21, 125–142. https://doi.org/10.1080/08919402.1914.10532671

Carlo, M. S., August, D., McLaughlin, B., Snow, C. E., Dressler, C., Lippman, D. N., … White, C. E. (2004). Closing the gap: Addressing the vocabulary needs of English-language learners in bilingual and mainstream classrooms. *Reading Research Quarterly*, 39(2), 188–215. https://doi.org/10.1598/RRQ.39.2.3

Carroll, J. B., Davies, P., & Richman, B. (1971). *The American heritage word frequency book*. New York, NY: American Heritage Publishing Co.

Cartmill, E., Armstrong, B. F., Gleitman, L. R., Goldin-Meadow, S., Medinac, T. N., & Trueswell, J. C. (2013). Quality of early parent input predicts child vocabulary 3 years later. *Proceedings of the National Academy of Sciences (PNAS)*, 110, 11278–11283. https://doi.org/10.1073/pnas.1309518110

Chall, J. S. (1987). Two vocabularies for reading: Recognition and meaning. In M. McKeown & M. Curtis (Eds.), *The nature of vocabulary acquisition* (pp. 7–17). Mahwah, NJ: Lawrence Erlbaum Associates.

Chung, T. M., & Nation, I. S. P. (2004). Identifying technical vocabulary. *System*, 32(2), 251–263. https://doi.org/10.1016/j.system.2003.11.008

Coffman, K. C., & Klinowski, D. (2020). The impact of penalties for wrong answers on the gender gap in test scores. *Proceedings of the National Academy of Sciences (PNAS)*, 117(16), 8794–8803. https://doi.org/10.1073/pnas.1920945117

Coxhead, A. (2004). Using a class vocabulary box: How, why, when, where and who. *Guidelines*, 26(2), 19–23.

Coxhead, A., & Bytheway, J. (2015). Learning vocabulary using two massive online resources: You will not blink. In D. Nunan & J. Richards (Eds.) *Learning beyond the classroom* (pp. 65–74). New York, NY: Routledge.

Coxhead, A., McLaughlin, E., & Reid, A. (2019). The development and application of a specialised word list: The case of fabrication. *Journal of Vocational Education & Training*, 71(2), 175–200. https://doi.org/10.1080/13636820.2018.1471094

Coxhead, A., Nation, I. S. P., & Sim, D. (2014). Creating and trialling six forms of the Vocabulary Size Test. *TESOLANZ Journal*, 22, 13–26.

Coxhead, A., Nation, P., & Sim, D. (2015). The vocabulary size of native speakers of English in New Zealand secondary schools. *New Zealand Journal of Educational Studies*, 50(1), 121–135. https://doi.org/10.1007/s40841-015-0002-3

Coxhead, A., Nation, P., Woods, L., & Sim, D. (2018). Group vs. individual: How administration procedure can affect vocabulary test scores. *New Zealand Studies in Applied Linguistics*, 24(2), 24–41.

Craig, H. (2011). Shakespeare's vocabulary: Myth and reality. *Shakespeare Quarterly*, 62(1), 53–74.

Dale, E. (1931). Evaluating Thorndike's word list. *Educational Research Bulletin*, 10(17), 451–457.

Dale, E., & O'Rourke, J. (1981). *The living word vocabulary*. Chicago, IL: World Book-Childcraft International.

Dale, E., & O'Rourke, J. (1976). *The living word vocabulary*. Chicago, IL: Field Enterprises Educational Corporation.

Dang, T. N. Y., & Webb, S. (2016). Evaluating lists of high-frequency words. *ITL-International Journal of Applied Linguistics*, 167, 132–158. https://doi.org/10.1075/itl.167.2.02dan

Dang, T. N. Y., Webb, S., & Coxhead, A. (2020). Evaluating lists of high-frequency words: Teachers' and learners' perspectives. *Language Teaching Research*, 1–25. https://doi.org/10.1177/1362168820911189

D'Anna, C. A., Zechmeister, E. B., & Hall, J. W. (1991). Toward a meaningful definition of vocabulary size. *Journal of Reading Behavior: A Journal of Literacy*, 23(1), 109–122. https://doi.org/10.1080/10862969109547729

Daulton, F. E. (2008). *Japan's built-in lexicon of English-based loanwords*. Clevedon: Multilingual Matters.

Deckner, D. F., Adamson, L. B., & Bakeman, R. (2006). Child and maternal contributions to shared reading: Effects on language and literacy development. *Journal of Applied Developmental Psychology*, 27, 31–41. https://doi.org/10.1016/j.appdev.2005.12.001

Diack, H. (1975a). *Standard literacy tests*. St. Albans: Hart-Davis Educational.

Diack, H. (1975b). *Test your own word power*. St. Albans: Paladin.

Dickinson, D. K., & Porche, M. V. (2011). Relation between language experiences in preschool classrooms and children's kindergarten and fourth-grade language and reading abilities. *Child Development*, 82(3), 870–886. https://doi.org/10.1111/j.1467-8624.2011.01576.x

Diller, K. C. (1978). *The language teaching controversy*. Rowley, MA: Newbury House.

Dolby, J. L., & Resnikoff, H. L. (1967). *The English word speculum*. The Hague: Mouton.

Doran, E. W. (1907). A study of vocabularies. *Pedagogical Seminary*, 14(4), 401–438.

Dowdall, N., Melendez-Torres, G. J., Murray, L., Gardner, F., Hartford, L., & Cooper, P. J. (2020). Shared picture book reading interventions for child language development: A systematic review and meta-analysis. *Child Development*, 91(2), e383–e399. https://doi.org/10.1111/cdev.13225

Duff, D., & Brydon, M. (2020). Estimates of individual differences in vocabulary size in English: how many words are needed to 'close the vocabulary gap'? *Journal of Research in Reading*, 43(4), 454–481.

Dunn, L. M. (1965). *Peabody Picture Vocabulary Test*. Minnesota, MN: American Guidance Service.

Dupuy, H. J. (1974). *The rationale, development and standardization of a basic word vocabulary test*. Washington, DC: US Govt Printing Office. https://doi.org/10.1037/e415662004-001

Elgort, I., & Coxhead, A. (2016). An introduction to the Vocabulary Size Test: Description, application and evaluation. In J. Fox & V. Aryadoust (Eds.), *Trends in language assessment research and practice* (pp. 286–301). Newcastle upon Tyne: Cambridge Scholars.

Elgort, I., Brysbaert, M., Stevens, M., & Van Asche, E. (2018). Contextual word learning during reading in a second language: An eye- movement study. *Studies in Second Language Acquisition*, 40(2), 341–366. https://doi.org/10.1017/S0272263117000109

Elley, W. B. (1989). Vocabulary acquisition from listening to stories. *Reading Research Quarterly*, 24(2), 174–187. https://doi.org/10.2307/747863

Eyckmans, J. (2004). *Measuring receptive vocabulary size*. Utrecht: Netherlands Graduate School of Linguistics.

Farkas, G., & Beron, K. (2004). The detailed age trajectory of oral vocabulary knowledge: Differences by class and race. *Social Science Research*, 33, 464–497. https://doi.org/10.1016/j.ssresearch.2003.08.001

Fernald, A., Marchman, V. A., & Weisleder, A. (2013). SES differences in language processing skill and vocabulary are evident at 18 months. *Developmental Science*, 16(2), 234–248. https://doi.org/10.1111/desc.12019

Francis, W. N., & Kucera, H. (1982). *Frequency analysis of English usage*. Boston, MA: Houghton Mifflin Company.

Funk & Wagnall. (1937). *New standard dictionary of the English language*. New York, NY: Funk & Wagnall.

Gale, M. C., & Gale, H. (1902). The vocabularies of three children in one family at two and three years of age. *Pedagogical Seminary*, 9, 422–435. https://doi.org/10.1080/08919402.1902.10534195

Gathercole, S. E., & Baddeley, A. D. (1993). *Working memory and language*. Hillsdale, NJ: Lawrence Erlbaum Associates.

Gerlach, F. M. (1917). Vocabulary studies. *Studies in education and psychology*, 1. Colorado Springs, CO: Colorado College.

Golinkoff, R. M., Hoff, E., Rowe, M. L., & Hirsh-Pasek, K. (2019). Language matters: Denying the existence of the 30-million-word gap has serious consequences. *Child Development*, 90(3), 985–992. https://doi.org/10.1111/cdev.13128

Goulden, R., Nation, P., & Read, J. (1990). How large can a receptive vocabulary be? *Applied Linguistics*, 11(4), 341–363. https://doi.org/10.1093/applin/11.4.341

Grant, L., & Nation, I. S. P. (2006). How many idioms are there in English? *ITL – International Journal of Applied Linguistics*, 151, 1–14. https://doi.org/10.2143/ITL.151.0.2015219

Grasby, K. L., Coventry, W. L., Byrne, B., & Olson, R. K. (2019). Little evidence that socio-economic status modifies heritability of literacy and numeracy in Australia. *Child Development*, 90(2), 623–637. https://doi.org/10.1111/cdev.12920

Gyllstad, H., Vilkaite, L., & Schmitt, N. (2015). Assessing vocabulary size through multiple-choice formats: Issues with guessing and sampling rates. *International Journal of Applied Linguistics*, 166(2), 276–303.

Hart, B., & Risley, T. R. (1995). *Meaningful differences in the everyday experience of young American children*. Baltimore, MD: Paul H. Brookes.

van Hees, J., & Nation, I. S. P. (2017). *What every primary school teacher should know about vocabulary?* Wellington: NZCER Press.

Heilig, M. R. (1913). A child's vocabulary. *Pedagogical Seminary*, 20, 1–16. https://doi.org/10.1080/08919402.1913.10534422

Heilmann, J., Weismer, S. E., Evans, J., & Hollar, C. (2005). Utility of the MacArthur–Bates Communicative Development Inventory in identifying language abilities of late-talking and typically developing toddlers. *American Journal of Speech-Language Pathology*, 14(1), 40–51. https://doi.org/10.1044/1058-0360(2005/006)

Herdan, G. (1960). *Type-token mathematics: A textbook of mathematical linguistics*. The Hague: Mouton.

Hill, L. A. (1969). Delayed copying. *ELT Journal*, 23(3), 238–239. https://doi.org/10.1093/elt/XXIII.3.238

Hoff, E. (2003). The specificity of environmental influence: Socio-economic status affects early vocabulary development. *Child Development*, 74(5), 1368–1378. https://doi.org/10.1111/1467-8624.00612

Hoff, E. (2006). How social contexts support and shape language development. *Developmental Review*, 26(1), 55–88. https://doi.org/10.1016/j.dr.2005.11.002

Hoff, E. (2013). Interpreting the early language trajectories of children from low-SES and language minority homes: Implications for closing achievement gaps. *Developmental Psychology*, 49(1), 4–4. https://doi.org/10.1037/a0027238

Hoff, E., & Naigles, L. (2002). How children use input to acquire a lexicon. *Child Development*, 73(2), 418–433. https://doi.org/10.1111/1467-8624.00415

Holden, E. S. (1875). On the number of words used in speaking and writing. *Bulletin of the Philosophical Society of Washington*, 2, 16–21, 28.

Holley, C. E. (1919). *First Annual Report of the Bureau of Educational Research*, University of Illinois.

Huibregtse, I., Admiraal, W., & Meara, P. (2002). Scores on a yes–no vocabulary test: Correction for guessing and response style. *Language Testing*, 19, 227–245. https://doi.org/10.1191/0265532202lt229oa

Hurtado, N., Marchman, V. A., & Fernald, A. (2008). Does input influence uptake? Links between maternal talk, processing speed and vocabulary size in Spanish-learning children. *Developmental Science*, 11(6), F31–F36. https://doi.org/10.1111/j.1467-7687.2008.00768.x

Huttenlocher, J., Haight, W., Bryk, A., Seltzer, M., & Lyons, T. (1991). Early vocabulary growth: Relation to language input and gender. *Developmental Psychology*, 27(2), 236–248. https://doi.org/10.1037/0012-1649.27.2.236

Joe, A. (1998). What effects do text-based tasks promoting generation have on incidental vocabulary acquisition? *Applied Linguistics*, 19(3), 357–377. https://doi.org/10.1093/applin/19.3.357

Jones, G., & Rowland, C. F. (2017). Diversity not quantity in caregiver speech: Using computational modeling to isolate the effects of the quantity and the diversity of the input on vocabulary growth. *Cognitive Psychology*, 98, 1–21. https://doi.org/10.1016/j.cogpsych.2017.07.002

Keuleers, E., & Brysbaert, M. (2010). Wuggy: A multilingual pseudoword generator. *Behavior Research Methods*, 42(3), 627–633. https://doi.org/10.3758/BRM.42.3.627

Keuleers, E., Stevens, M., Mandera, P., & Brysbaert, M. (2015). Word knowledge in the crowd: Measuring vocabulary size and word prevalence in a massive online experiment. *The Quarterly Journal of Experimental Psychology*, 68(8), 1665–1692. https://doi.org/10.1080/17470218.2015.1022560

Kirkpatrick, E. A. (1891). Number of words in an ordinary vocabulary. *Science*, 18, 446, 107–108. https://doi.org/10.1126/science.ns-18.446.107-a

Kirkpatrick, E. A. (1907). A vocabulary test. *Popular Science Monthly*, 70, 157–164.

König, J., Calude, A., & Coxhead, A. (2019). Using character-grams to automatically generate pseudowords and how to evaluate them. *Applied Linguistics*. First view, 0/0: 1–24. https://doi.org/10.1093/applin/amz045

Kremmel, B., & Schmitt, N. (2016). What do various item formats tell us about learners' ability to employ words? Interpreting vocabulary test scores. *Language Assessment Quarterly*, 13(4), 377–392. https://doi.org/10.1080/15434303.2016.1237516

Labov, W. (1973). The logic of non-standard English. In N. Keddie (Ed.), *Tinker, tailor ... The myth of cultural deprivation* (pp. 21–66). Harmondsworth: Penguin Books.

Langenbeck, M. (1914). A study of a five-year-old child. *Pedagogical Seminary*, 22, 65–88. https://doi.org/10.1080/08919402.1915.10533950

Larson, M. (2019). Estimating the vocabulary sizes of learners around the world. Presentation at IALLT 2019 (International Association for Language Learning Technology), Eugene, Oregon. <http://www.vocabularysize.net/iallt2019/iallt.html>

Laufer, B., Elder, C., Hill, K., & Congdon, P. (2004). Size and strength: Do we need both to measure vocabulary knowledge? *Language Testing*, 21(2), 202–226. https://doi.org/10.1191/0265532204lt277oa

Laufer, B., & Goldstein, Z. (2004). Testing vocabulary knowledge: Size, strength, and computer adaptiveness. *Language Learning*, 54(3), 399–436. https://doi.org/10.1111/j.0023-8333.2004.00260.x

Lemhöfer, K., & Broersma, M. (2012). Introducing LexTALE: A quick and valid Lexical Test for Advanced Learners of English. *Behavior Research Methods*, 44(2), 325–343. https://doi.org/10.3758/s13428-011-0146-0

Liu, O. L., Bridgeman, B., & Adler, R. M. (2012). Measuring learning outcomes in higher education: Motivation matters. *Educational Researcher*, 41(9), 352–362. https://doi.org/10.3102/0013189X12459679

Liu, O. L., Rios, J. A., & Borden, V. (2015). The effects of motivational instruction on college students' performance on low-stakes assessment. *Educational Assessment*, 20(1), 79–94. https://doi.org/10.1080/10627197.2015.1028618

Lonigan, C. J., & Milburn, T. F. (2017). Identifying the dimensionality of oral language skills of children with typical development in preschool through fifth grade. *Journal of Speech, Language, and Hearing Research*, 60, 2185–2198. https://doi.org/10.1044/2017_JSLHR-L-15-0402

Lorge, I., & Chall, J. (1963). Estimating the size of vocabularies of children and adults: an analysis of methodological issues. *Journal of Experimental Education*, 32, 147–157. https://doi.org/10.1080/00220973.1963.11010819

Macalister, J., & Nation, I. S. P. (2020). *Language curriculum design*. New York, NY: Routledge.

Mancilla-Martinez, J., Pan, B. A., & Vagh, S. B. (2011). Assessing the productive vocabulary of Spanish-English bilingual toddlers from low-income families. *Applied Psycholinguistics*, 32(2), 333–357. https://doi.org/10.1017/S0142716410000433

Mastin, J. D., & Vogt, P. (2016). Infant engagement and early vocabulary development: A naturalistic observation study of Mozambican infants from 1;1 to 2;1. *Journal of Child Language*, 43, 235–264. https://doi.org/10.1017/S0305000915000148

Mateer, F. (1908). The vocabulary of a four year old boy. *Pedagogical Seminary*, 15, 63–74. https://doi.org/10.1080/08919402.1908.10534115

McDonald, K., & Asaba, M. (2015). "I Don't Know" use and guessing on the bilingual Japanese Vocabulary Size Test: A preliminary report. *Vocabulary Learning and Instruction*, 4(1), 16–25.

Meara, P., & Jones, G. (1987). Tests of vocabulary size in English as a foreign language. *Polyglot*, 8, (Fiche 1).

Mochida, A., & Harrington, M. (2006). The Yes/No test as a measure of receptive vocabulary knowledge. *Language Testing*, 23(1), 73–98. https://doi.org/10.1191/0265532206lt321oa

Mol, S., Bus, A., de Jong, M., & Smeets, D. (2008). Added value of dialogic parent-child book readings: A meta-analysis. *Early Education and Development*, 19(1), 7–26. https://doi.org/10.1080/10409280701838603

Nagy, W. E., & Anderson, R. C. (1984). How many words are there in printed school English? *Reading Research Quarterly*, 19, 304–330. https://doi.org/10.2307/747823

Nagy, W. E., Herman, P., & Anderson, R. C. (1985). Learning words from context. *Reading Research Quarterly*, 20(2), 233–253. https://doi.org/10.2307/747758

Nation, I. S. P. (1993). Using dictionaries to estimate vocabulary size: essential, but rarely followed, procedures. *Language Testing*, 10(1), 27–40.

Nation, I. S. P. (2000). Learning vocabulary in lexical sets: dangers and guidelines. *TESOL Journal*, 9(2), 6–10.

Nation, I. S. P. (2006). How large a vocabulary is needed for reading and listening? *Canadian Modern Language Review*, 63(1), 59–82. https://doi.org/10.3138/cmlr.63.1.59

Nation, I. S. P. (2007a). The four strands. *Innovation in Language Learning and Teaching*, 1(1), 1–12. https://doi.org/10.2167/illt039.0

Nation, I. S. P. (2007b). Fundamental issues in modelling and assessing vocabulary knowledge. In H. Daller, J. Milton, & J. Treffers-Daller (Eds.), *Modelling and assessing vocabulary knowledge* (pp. 35–43). Cambridge: Cambridge University Press. https://doi.org/10.1017/CBO9780511667268.004

Nation, I. S. P. (2013). *Learning vocabulary in another language* (2nd ed.). Cambridge: Cambridge University Press. https://doi.org/10.1017/CBO9781139858656

Nation, I. S. P. (2016). *Making and using word lists for language learning and testing*. Amsterdam: John Benjamins. https://doi.org/10.1075/z.208

Nation, I. S. P., & Anthony, L. (2016). Measuring vocabulary size. In E. Hinkel (Ed.), *Handbook of research in second language teaching and learning*, Vol. III. New York, NY: Routledge. https://doi.org/10.4324/9781315716893-26

Nation, I. S. P., & Beglar, D. (2007). A vocabulary size test. *The Language Teacher*, 31(7), 9–13.

Nation, I. S. P., & Crabbe, D. (1991). A survival language learning syllabus for foreign travel. *System*, 19(3), 191–201. https://doi.org/10.1016/0346-251X(91)90044-P

Nation, I. S. P., & Macalister, J. (2021). *Teaching ESL/EFL reading and writing*. New York, NY: Routledge.

Nation, I. S. P., & Webb, S. (2011). *Researching and analyzing vocabulary*. Boston, MA: Heinle Cengage Learning.

Neher, H. L. (1918). Measuring the vocabulary of high school pupils. *School and Society*, 8, 355–359.

Nguyen, L. T. C., & Nation, I. S. P. (2011). A bilingual vocabulary size test of English for Vietnamese learners. *RELC Journal*, 42(1), 86–99. https://doi.org/10.1177/0033688210390264

O'Neil, A. F., Abedi, J., Miyoshi, J., & Mastergeorge, A. (2005). Monetary incentives for low-stakes tests. *Educational Assessment*, 10(3), 185–208. https://doi.org/10.1207/s15326977ea1003_3

Pan, B. A., Rowe, M. L., Singer, J. D., & Snow, C. E. (2005). Maternal correlates of growth in toddler vocabulary production in low-income families. *Child Development*, 76(4), 763–782.

Parent, K. (2012). The most frequent English homonyms. *RELC Journal*, 43(1), 69–81. https://doi.org/10.1177/0033688212439356

Paul, P. V., Stallman, A. C., & O'Rourke, J. P. (1990). Using three test formats to assess good and poor readers' word knowledge. *Technical Report No. 509 Center for the Study of Reading, University of Illinois at Urbana-Champaign.*
Pellicer-Sanchez, A., & Schmitt, N. (2012). Scoring Yes-No vocabulary tests: Reaction time vs non-word approaches. *Language Testing*, 29(4), 489–509. https://doi.org/10.1177/0265532212438053
Pelsma, J. R. (1914). A child's vocabulary and its development. *Pedagogical Seminary*, 17, 329–369.
Pollard-Durodola, S. D., Gonzalez, J. E., Simmons, D. C., Kwok, O., Taylor, A. B., Davis, M. J., ... Simmons, L. (2011). The effects of an intensive shared book-reading intervention for preschool children at risk for vocabulary delay. *Exceptional Children*, 77(2), 161–181. https://doi.org/10.1177/001440291107700202
Quero, B. (2015). Estimating the vocabulary size of L1 Spanish ESP learners and the vocabulary load of medical textbooks (Unpublished doctoral dissertation), Victoria University of Wellington, New Zealand.
Read, J. (2000). *Assessing vocabulary*. Cambridge: Cambridge University Press. https://doi.org/10.1017/CBO9780511732942
Richards, B. J., & Malvern, D. D. (1997). *Quantifying lexical diversity in the study of language development*. Reading: University of Reading.
Rosenthal, R. (1987). *Judgement studies: Design, analysis, and meta-analysis*. Cambridge: Cambridge University Press. https://doi.org/10.1017/CBO9780511527807
Rowe, E. C., & Rowe, H. (1913). The vocabulary of a child at four and six years of age. *Pedagogical Seminary*, 20, 187–208. https://doi.org/10.1080/08919402.1913.10534441
Rowe, M. L. (2012). A longitudinal investigation of the role of quantity and quality of child-directed speech in vocabulary development. *Child Development*, 83(3), 1762–1774. https://doi.org/10.1111/j.1467-8624.2012.01805.x
Rowe, M. L. (2018). Understanding socio-economic differences in parents' speech to children. *Child Development Perspectives*, 12(2), 122–127. https://doi.org/10.1111/cdep.12271
Rowe, M. L., & Goldin-Meadow, S. (2009). Differences in early gesture explain SES disparities in child vocabulary size at school entry. *Science*, 323, 951–953. https://doi.org/10.1126/science.1167025
Rowe, M. L., Raudenbush, S. W., & Goldin-Meadow, S. (2012). The pace of vocabulary growth helps predict later vocabulary skill. *Child Development*, 82(3), 508–525. https://doi.org/10.1111/j.1467-8624.2011.01710.x
Schmitt, N. (2019). Understanding vocabulary acquisition, instruction, and assessment: A research agenda. *Language Teaching*, 52, 261–274.
Schmitt, N. (2010). *Researching vocabulary: A vocabulary research manual*. Houndmills: Palgrave Macmillan. https://doi.org/10.1057/9780230293977
Schmitt, N., & Schmitt, D. (2014). A reassessment of frequency and vocabulary size in L2 vocabulary teaching. *Language Teaching*, 47(4), 484–503.
Schmitt, N., Schmitt, D., & Clapham, C. (2001). Developing and exploring the behaviour of two new versions of the Vocabulary Levels Test. *Language Testing* 18(1), 55–88. https://doi.org/10.1177/026553220101800103
Scott, J. A., & Nagy, W. E. (2004). Developing word consciousness. In J. F. Baumann & E. J. Kame'enui (Eds.), *Vocabulary instruction: Research to practice* (pp. 201–217). New York, NY: Guilford Press.

Seashore, R. H., & Eckerson, L. D. (1940). The measurement of individual differences in general English vocabularies. *Journal of Educational Psychology*, 3l, 14–38.

Segal, C. (2012). Working when no one is watching: Motivation, test scores, and economic success. *Management Science*, 58(8), 1438–1457. https://doi.org/10.1287/mnsc.1110.1509

Senechal, M., Pagan, S., Lever, R., & Ouellette, G. P. (2008). Relations among the frequency of shared reading and 4-year-old children's vocabulary, morphological and syntax comprehension, and narrative skills. *Early Education and Development*, 19(1), 27–44. https://doi.org/10.1080/10409280701838710

Shneidman, L. J., Arroyo, M. E., Levine, S. C., & Goldin-Meadow, S. (2013). What counts as effective input for word learning? *Journal of Child Language*, 40, 672–686. https://doi.org/10.1017/S0305000912000141

Schmitt, N. (2019). Understanding vocabulary acquisition, instruction, and assessment: A research agenda. *Language Teaching*, 52, 261–274. https://doi.org/10.1017/S0261444819000053

Schmitt, N., & Schmitt, D. (2014). A reassessment of frequency and vocabulary size in L2 vocabulary teaching. *Language Teaching*, 47(4), 484–503. https://doi.org/10.1017/S0261444812000018

Singer, T., Verhaeghen, P., Ghisletta, P., Lindenberger, U., & Baltes, P. B. (2003). The fate of cognition in very old age: Six-year longitudinal findings in the Berlin Aging Study (BASE). *Psychology and Aging*, 18(2), 318–331. https://doi.org/10.1037/0882-7974.18.2.318

Sorell, C. J. (2012). Zipf's law and vocabulary. In C. A. Chapelle (Ed.), *Encyclopaedia of applied linguistics*. Oxford: Wiley-Blackwell. https://doi.org/10.1002/9781405198431.wbeal1302

Sperry, D. E., Sperry, L. L., & Miller, P. J. (2019a). Language does matter: But there is more to language than vocabulary and directed speech. *Child Development*, 90(3), 993–997. https://doi.org/10.1111/cdev.13125

Sperry, D. E., Sperry, L. L., & Miller, P. J. (2019b). Reexamining the verbal environments of children from different socio-economic backgrounds. *Child Development*, 90(4), 1303–1318. https://doi.org/10.1111/cdev.13072

Stauffer, R. G. (1942). A study of prefixes in the Thorndike list to establish a list of prefixes that that should be taught in elementary school. *Journal of Educational Research*, 35, 453–458. https://doi.org/10.1080/00220671.1942.10881100

Stewart, J. (2014). Do multiple-choice options inflate estimates of vocabulary size on the VST? *Language Assessment Quarterly*, 11(3), 271–282. https://doi.org/10.1080/15434303.2014.922977

Stoeckel, T., Bennett, P., & McLean, S. (2016). Is "I don't know" a viable answer choice on the Vocabulary Size Test? *TESOL Quarterly*, 50(4), 965–975. https://doi.org/10.1002/tesq.325

Stoeckel, T., McLean, S., & Nation, I. S. P. (2020). Limitations of size and levels tests of written receptive vocabulary knowledge. *Studies in Second Language Acquisition*, 1–20. https://doi.org/10.1017/S027226312000025X

Stoeckel, T., Stewart, J., McLean, S., Ishii, T., Kramer, B., & Matsumoto, Y. (2019). The relationship of four variants of the Vocabulary Size Test to a criterion measure of meaning recall vocabulary knowledge. *System*, 87, 1–14. https://doi.org/10.1016/j.system.2019.102161

Stubbe, R. (2012). Do pseudoword false alarm rates and overestimation rates in Yes/No vocabulary tests change with Japanese university students' English ability levels? *Language Testing*, 29(4), 471–488. https://doi.org/10.1177/0265532211433033

Stubbe, R., & Stewart, J. (2012). Optimizing scoring formulas for Yes/No vocabulary tests with linear models. *Shiken Research Bulletin*, 16(2), 2–7.

Suskind, D. L., Leffel, K. R., Graf, E., Hernandez, M. W., Gunderson, E. A., Sapolich, S. G., … Levine, S. C. (2016). A parent-directed language intervention for children of low socio-economic status: A randomized controlled pilot study. *Journal of Child Language*, 43, 366–406. https://doi.org/10.1017/S0305000915000033

Sutarsyah, C., Nation, P., & Kennedy, G. (1994). How useful is EAP vocabulary for ESP? A corpus based study. *RELC Journal*, 25(2), 34–50. https://doi.org/10.1177/003368829402500203

Tegge, F. (2017). The lexical coverage of popular songs in English language teaching. *System*, 67, 87–98. https://doi.org/10.1016/j.system.2017.04.016

Terman, L. M. (1916). *The Measurement of Intelligence*. Boston: Houghton-Mifflin.

Thorndike, E. L. (1921a). *The teacher's word book*. New York, NY: Teachers College Columbia University.

Thorndike, E. L. (1921b). Word knowledge in the elementary school. *Teachers College Record*, 22, 334–370.

Thorndike, E. L. (1924). The vocabularies of school pupils. In J. Carelton Bell (Ed.), *Contributions to Education* (pp. 69–76). New York, NY: World Book Co.

Thorndike, E. L., & Lorge, I. (1944). *The teacher's word book of 30,000 words*. New York, NY: Teachers College Columbia University.

Tyler, A., & Nagy, W. (1989). The acquisition of English derivational morphology. *Journal of Memory and Language*, 28, 649–667. https://doi.org/10.1016/0749-596X(89)90002-8

Uhrbrock, R. S. (1935). The vocabulary of a five-year-old. *Educational Research Bulletin*, 14(44), 85–97.

Verhaeghen, P. (2003). Aging and vocabulary scores: A meta-analysis. *Psychology and Aging*, 18(2), 332–339. https://doi.org/10.1037/0882-7974.18.2.332

Waring, R., & Takaki, M. (2003). At what rate do learners learn and retain new vocabulary from reading a graded reader? *Reading in a Foreign Language*, 15(2), 130–163.

Webb, S. (2010). A corpus driven study of the potential for vocabulary learning through watching movies. *International Journal of Corpus Linguistics*, 15(4), 497–519. https://doi.org/10.1075/ijcl.15.4.03web

Webb, S., & Nation, I. S. P. (2017). *How vocabulary is learned*. Oxford: Oxford University Press.

Webb, S., & Rodgers, M. P. H. (2009a). The lexical coverage of movies. *Applied Linguistics*, 30(3), 407–427. https://doi.org/10.1093/applin/amp010

Webb, S., & Rodgers, M. P. H. (2009b). The vocabulary demands of television programs. *Language Learning*, 59(2), 335–366. https://doi.org/10.1111/j.1467-9922.2009.00509.x

Webb, S., Sasao, Y., & Ballance, O. (2017). The updated Vocabulary Levels Test. *ITL International Journal of Applied Linguistics*, 168(1), 33–69. https://doi.org/10.1075/itl.168.1.02web

Wei, Z., & Nation, P. (2013). The word part technique: A very useful vocabulary teaching technique. *Modern English Teacher*, 22(1), 12–16.

Weisleder, A., & Fernald, A. (2013). Talking to children matters: Early language experience strengthens processing and builds vocabulary. *Psychological Science*, 24(11), 2143–2152. https://doi.org/10.1177/0956797613488145

West, M. (1955). *A general service list of English words*. London: Longman.

Whipple, G. M., & Whipple, M. (1909). The vocabulary of a three-year-old boy with some interpretive comments. *Pedagogical Seminary*, 16(1), 1–22. https://doi.org/10.1080/08919402.1909.10532566

White, T. G., Power, M. A., & White, S. (1989). Morphological analysis: Implications for teaching and understanding vocabulary growth. *Reading Research Quarterly* 24, 283–304. https://doi.org/10.2307/747771

Wigfield, A., & Eccles, J. (2000). Expectancy-value theory of achievement motivation. *Contemporary Educational Psychology*, 25, 68–81. https://doi.org/10.1006/ceps.1999.1015
de Wilde, V., Brysbaert, M., & Eyckmans, J. (2019). Learning English through out-of-school exposure. Which levels of language proficiency are attained and which types of input are important? *Bilingualism: Language and Cognition*, 23, 171–185. https://doi.org/10.1017/S1366728918001062
Willard, A. I., Busch, J. T. A., Cullum, K. A., Letourneau, S. M., Sobel, D. M., Callanan, M., & Legare, C. H. (2019). Explain this, explore that: A study of parent–child interaction in a children's museum. *Child Development*, 90(5), e598–e617. https://doi.org/10.1111/cdev.13232
Williams, H. M. (1932). Some problems of sampling in vocabulary tests. *Journal of Experimental Education*, 1, 131–133. https://doi.org/10.1080/00220973.1932.11009895
Wise, S. L., & DeMars, C. E. (2010). Examinee noneffort and the validity of program assessment results. *Educational Assessment*, 15(1), 27–41. https://doi.org/10.1080/10627191003673216
Wise, S. L., & DeMars, C. E. (2005). Low examinee effort in low-stakes assessment: Problems and potential solutions. *Educational Assessment*, 10(1), 1–17. https://doi.org/10.1207/s15326977ea1001_1
Zhang, X. (2013). The 'I Don't Know' option in the Vocabulary Size Test. *TESOL Quarterly*, 47, 790–811. https://doi.org/10.1002/tesq.98

Author index

Subject index